I DIDN'T ASK
TO BE BORN

I DIDN'T ASK
TO BE BORN
(BUT I'M GLAD I WAS)

BILL
COSBY

Illustrations by George Booth

CENTER
STREET

NEW YORK BOSTON NASHVILLE

Page 59—From the Joseph A. Ferko website: Since 1922, the Joseph A.
Ferko String Band has been entertaining audiences the world over. A
participant in Philadelphia's annual Mummers Parade, The Ferko String
Band boasts the most successful record in the history of the parade.

Page 114—American historian Howard Zinn (August 24, 1922–January
27, 2010) was a Professor of Political Science at Boston University for over
20 years and a noted author and intellectual.

Center Street
Hachette Book Group
237 Park Avenue
New York, NY 10017

www.centerstreet.com

Printed in the United States of America

RRD-C

First Edition: November 2011
10 9 8 7 6 5 4 3 2 1

Center Street is a division of Hachette Book Group, Inc.
The Center Street name and logo are trademarks of
Hachette Book Group, Inc.

The Hachette Speakers Bureau provides a wide range
of authors for speaking events. To find out more, go to
www.hachettespeakersbureau.com or call (866) 376-6591.

The publisher is not responsible for websites (or their content)
that are not owned by the publisher.

Library of Congress Cataloging-in-Publication Data

Cosby, Bill, 1937–
   I didn't ask to be born (but I'm glad I was) / Bill Cosby. — 1st ed.
    p. cm.
   ISBN 978-0-89296-920-3
   1. Cosby, Bill, 1937–   2. American wit and humor.
3. Comedians—United States—Biography.   I. Title.
   PN2287.C632A3 2011
   729.702'8092—dc22
   [B]
                                                        2011017071

DEDICATION AND ACKNOWLEDGMENTS

Here are my dedication and acknowledgments. Which are almost like a will, except you don't give any money or property away.

I dedicate this book to Dorothy Height, whom I'm sure was put in the E-ZPass lane to Heaven. And I mean the whole book. I mean the jacket. I mean the page numbers. The dog-ears. All of it. Everything. Even when it goes into paperback.

To James Moody for his sax solo on "I'm in the Mood for Love," which inspired Eddie Jefferson to write the lyrics for what became "Moody's Mood for Love," made popular by the singer King Pleasure and which went on to become the national anthem of puberty. Thank you for providing the background music (in my mind) for Bernadette.

To Robert Culp. I don't want to say you were a genius because that's such a usual thing to say. Whatever it was that you had, Bob, you were on the positive side of gray matter. The way you directed and rewrote *Hickey & Boggs* and turned it into a respected piece. How you played the wonderful Hoby Gilman in a black-and-white Western. When we were doing *I Spy* there were times when people would hear us ad-lib names like Stanley and Fred C. Dobbs. Stanley from Laurel and Hardy and Fred C. Dobbs, the character Humphrey Bogart played in *The Treasure of the Sierra Madre*. And there was your occasional side-of-the-mouth Sheldon Leonard imitation, which sounded like W. C. Fields, Kelly Robinson, and Alexander Scott. I remember the things we talked about and laughed about and smiled about.

I'll see you later.

To D. L. Wilder for the inspiration to write about Bernadette Johnson's father.

AUTHOR'S NOTE

All of my performances and writings have been inspired by my experiences, which, I believe, give an honest and truthful picture of life. My observations are not bread crumbs. They do not dissolve. They are on record, on film, printed in books, and found on the Internet. I am happy to share them. For this I was born. And I'm glad I was. Although in my early years, I was pitiful.

CONTENTS

I DIDN'T ASK
TO BE BORN

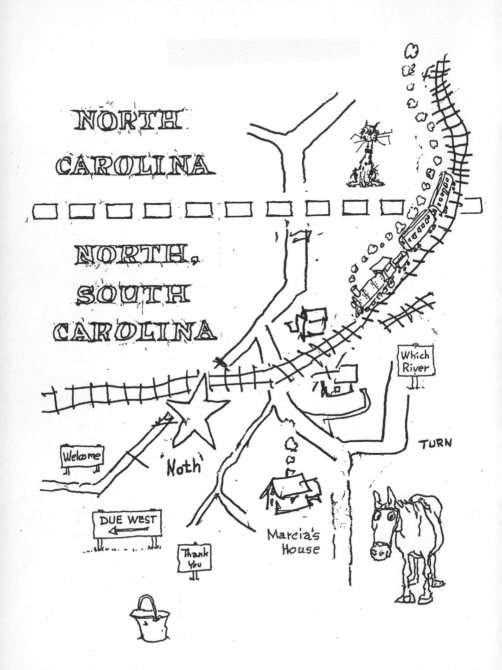

ME AND MARCIA:
YOU BET YOUR LIFE

Ladies and gentlemen, what you are about to read is a perfect example of the perfect guest on a talk show. At the time of this interview, I believed strongly that I had found the format for the rest of my career. The ratings would prove me wrong, I'm sorry to say.

However, after thousands of hours of interviews of human beings who have something unusual in their lives—don't we all—this young lady, with her southern accent and completely natural delivery, represents the most perfect guest and the most enjoyable. Not narcissistic. Not arrogant. Just the most fantastic guest.

And so I am proud to present to you my most perfect moment as a television talk show host. (I leave out the game show part because I think that's what caused the cancellation.)

Bill Cosby: Marcia Brody.

Marcia Brody: Hello.

Bill Cosby: How are you?

Marcia Brody: I'm fine.

Bill Cosby: Cheltenham, Pennsylvania.

Marcia Brody: That's right.

Bill Cosby: Born?

Marcia Brody: No, I'm originally from North, South Carolina.

Bill Cosby: That's what I thought. Yeah, I don't know too many people from Cheltenham that talk like that.

Marcia Brody: Well, I lived over twenty-five years down south.

Bill Cosby: What was the name of the place?

Marcia Brody: North.

Bill Cosby: Nowith?

Marcia Brody: No. N-o-r-t-h. North. It's in South Carolina. In South Carolina, it's a little town called Due West. And North—

Bill Cosby: Wait, wait, slow down. In what—North Carolina?

Marcia Brody: No, South Carolina. In South Carolina, there's a little town called Due West. And North is ninety miles southeast of Due West. That's right. North is south of the capital, Columbia. You understand?

Bill Cosby: I was doing fine until you came out here. Then you started talking and I got lost. And I'm not in a car and I didn't care to go anywhere. Now you have me someplace I have no idea where I am. I'm in the town North south of Due West.

Marcia Brody: No, no.

Bill Cosby: Well, where am I?

Marcia Brody: It's North, comma, South Carolina.

Bill Cosby: In North South Carolina.

Marcia Brody: North, comma, South Carolina.

Bill Cosby: Comma is the name?

Marcia Brody: No, no! You put a comma in between North and South Carolina.

Bill Cosby: I'm in the state of South Carolina...

Marcia Brody: Right, right.

Bill Cosby: But I'm in a city called North?

Marcia Brody: It's not a city; it's a town.

Bill Cosby: A town. Okay, let me ask you this. Where is the railroad?

Marcia Brody: Oh, the railroad is right in the middle of the town.

Bill Cosby: That's right. Now, stop there. Now, where are the black people?

Marcia Brody: I don't know. I mean they're all around, I guess. I don't know.

Bill Cosby: They're not all around. They're either on this side of the track or that side of the track. Are we Due North or southwest?

Marcia Brody: You're in North.

Bill Cosby: I'm in North.

Marcia Brody: Right, South Carolina.

Bill Cosby: Here we go again.

Marcia Brody: Anyway...

Bill Cosby: No, there's no anyway. I'm sitting in my car and I'm lost. I want to find my people. And you're trying to give me directions. Now, okay, let's put it this way. Where is the river?

Marcia Brody: Which river?

Bill Cosby: Is there an East River?

Marcia Brody: I don't know.

Bill Cosby: Is there a West River?

Marcia Brody: I don't even know where the river is.

Bill Cosby: Now I know how you wound up in Cheltenham.

Marcia Brody: Anyway, I come from a family of seven children and five of us are living and we're all grandparents. So we all like to know what's happening with everybody else. So I put out a family paper three times a year.

Bill Cosby: Do you have a sports column?

Marcia Brody: No, but you'll be the headlines on my next paper. Oh, my goodness! Yeah!

Bill Cosby: Why don't you just send them the video?

Marcia Brody: What video? What kind of video?

Bill Cosby: The video of this show. You make a video of it.

Marcia Brody: I don't have a video of it.

Bill Cosby: No. You're correct. We don't have one yet.

Marcia Brody: Yeah. What? Are you making one?

Bill Cosby: Yeah. I'm going to make a video for you. And then you can—

Marcia Brody: Oh. Well, I have three sisters in South Carolina and I have a brother in Mississippi.

Bill Cosby: You got a pen?

Marcia Brody: Three sisters in South Carolina. A brother in Mississippi.

Bill Cosby: What part of South Carolina?

Marcia Brody: One's in Charleston. One's in Beaufort. One's in Bishopville. Then I have a brother in Mississippi.

Bill Cosby: What part?

Marcia Brody: Oxford. You want to send it...you want to send it to all my nieces and nephews?

Bill Cosby: No, no, it's too many of them. I'm not sending to the grandchildren either. See, I'll just make it up for the ones in Charleston, Beaufort, and Bishop.

Marcia Brody: Bishop*ville*.

Bill Cosby: Okay.

Marcia Brody: And don't forget my brother in Mississippi.

Bill Cosby: No, Oxford, I got that.

Marcia Brody: Okay, then how about my son in New Jersey? He lives near Trenton.

Bill Cosby: How did you get somebody in New Jersey?

Marcia Brody: Oh, he's the one that made me the grandmother.

Bill Cosby: Ah! How do you like that?

Marcia Brody: Oh, it's nice. Really is nice.

Bill Cosby: They drop the baby off?

Marcia Brody: Where?

And so there you have it. The perfect onetime conversation. And I say "onetime conversation" because I don't know what other subjects she could discuss if we brought her back. And, in fact, nobody said — maybe because the show didn't last that long — we've got to have her back on the show. Then she would come back and it would be a nightmare because she would not be as wonderful as before. What she did the first time created an unbeatable mark, whether you're high-jumping or doing the limbo.

But I do believe it is great that we did this one thing together.

BERNADETTE

Those of you who are from, like, zero up to about forty-five years old, I'm going to tell you a story that happened in the fifties. It's about a girl named Bernadette Johnson. But I want you to know I'm not bragging.

When old people start to talk about "their time," there is a tendency for young people to doze. And young people always say:

That was before my time.

But I just want young people to know we're not bragging about what we had to do in those days. You're not bragging when you talk about having to walk five miles in eight-foot snowdrifts. There's nobody on the face of the earth born who woke up knowing that he or she had to walk five miles in eight feet of snow, with no shoes, who said:

Oh goody! I'll have something to tell young people.

No, you don't do that. You say the same thing anybody else would say:

Why me?

And your parents say:

Because I had you.

Now, when I was a kid, there was no law protecting us from old people. Let me put it to you this way. There was no saying:

Well, he's having a bad day.

There was no psychologist, no psychiatrist, that anybody paid attention to, because crazy people didn't want to be crazy. See, crazy people get mad if you say they're crazy. They didn't want you to know they were crazy, so they were always trying to hide the fact that they were crazy. But everybody knew they were crazy.

Now, when I reminisce about the forties, I repeat, I am not bragging. I'm just relating my experience growing up and looking back on it today. It would be the same if Charles Lindbergh sat here to talk about his flight across the Atlantic in a single-engine plane. He's not bragging; he's telling the truth. He would've loved to have had a twin-engine jet, with instruments, and radar, and all of that, so he could've gone to sleep.

When I was thirteen, there was a girl, many girls, actually, and they always seemed to be armed with some kind of question I wasn't ready for. One girl, she was just gorgeous. So I went up to her. Now, in those days you would go up to a girl and ask:

Would you like to go out with me?

You didn't need to do much more than that. Just walk up and say:

Would you like to go out with me?

We were thirteen so she would just say yes or no. Even if she said yes, you weren't going to do much, because girls were taught to make the male behave. If you tried anything, they'd say:

Stop!

It was like Olympic boxing.

Stop!

Yes, okay.

And our job was to try to sneak up on her, so that she didn't really think we were touching or anything. But she would still say:

Stop!

And you would stop.

So I went up to this one girl and said, "Would you like to go out with me?"

And she said, "Why do you want to go out with me?"

I said the only thing I was armed with:

"Because I love you."

And I did. I did love her. I really did. That's why I told her I loved her.

She asked me, "What is love?"

Now, this is a thirteen-year-old girl, asking me "What is love?" I'm not prepared. I just thought I would use the highest form of a feeling for her and she would "go out with me." What's wrong with her? Asking me "What is love?"

"It means that I love you," I finally said.

"But what *is* love?"

"I just love you."

And I was getting mad at her. I don't love her anymore. Never mind. You ask all these questions, man.

When I turned fourteen, there was another girl. She was beautiful. One of the really great-looking ones, and like all the great-looking girls, she had an ugly friend. So you had to talk to the ugly friend first and get permission to talk to the great-looking one. Eventually I got past the ugly friend and was able to talk to the great-looking one, and the first thing I said to her was "I would like to go out with you."

She said—very nicely, I remember—she said, "I would like for this to be platonic."

I didn't know what the word meant. All I knew was that she said it like it was something she wanted. So I said, "Okay, great."

I went home and asked my father, "What does the word 'platonic' mean?"

My father said, "It means y'not gonna get any."

"Get any what?" I wanted to know.

"Good," my father said, "you won't miss it."

When I turned fifteen, I figured out what I was missing. And so, at the age of fifteen, there's a whole lot of lying going on. Boys lying about who got some. They used to call it "some" in those days.

Did you get some?

Yeah, I got some.

Then you'd help your friend lie and he would help you lie.

You see him get some?

Yeah, I saw him when he got some.

Fifteen years old. When you turned fifteen, you'd give twenty cents to Bobby Franklin, who was eighteen. Bobby Franklin would go to the drugstore and get you a condom, which you then put in your wallet and kept in your back pocket. After a while, it makes a ring, a round indentation in the leather. If somebody asked you:

Have you ever had any?

You don't even answer. You just take out your wallet and show them the round dent in the leather.

Ten years later, I think I was about twenty-five, I found my old wallet in my mother's house, in my bedroom, in the dresser drawer. When I took out the condom and opened it up, the thing just escaped, like a bird. It was so happy to be open, to fly away. Nothing but dust. Rubber dust that just exploded.

Yeah, I got some.

Oh yes. We were talking about Bernadette Johnson. Bernadette Johnson was *fine*. When somebody said Bernadette Johnson? Nothing else to say. She was *fine*. This word defines everything any fifteen-year-old boy would want in a girl.

Fine.

When you're fifteen, sixteen years old, you say the word in a very specific way. You would narrow your eyes—the eyelids, you would narrow them. Not closed, but just narrow. And as you said it, the word would affect the facial muscles so that you made a face that would cause some people to think you were in great pain. Which actually, in a way, is the truth. The eyes are narrowed, and the face really does look like it's in pain—a quiet facial reaction to pain.

Fine.

Pain. Not a bad smell. Pain. And then it's like your head is on an axis. Your head swivels, goes from side to side, moving only about a quarter of an inch, then coming back about a quarter of an inch in the other direction. And you have the top teeth biting down, gently over the bottom lip, and you're letting air come out. Sort of like listening to the most famous recording of "Body and Soul" by Coleman Hawkins—Coleman Hawkins on the tenor saxophone, blowing and hearing air before the note.

Fine.

So when you talked about Bernadette, you started with:

She ...

That's when the eyes narrow. And the *e* in "she" becomes three *e*'s.

Sheee...

And then the head goes up as if you were sending your face to Heaven.

Sheee iiisss...

And then your face drops about two inches down, and the whole head drops down too.

Fine!

Now, it's not just a male thing, being afraid to speak up for fear of being rejected. But in those days, girls were taught that it was "unladylike" to approach a boy.

You will not—I don't care how much you care for him, or how crazy you are about him—ever go up to him and say something.

So being a fifteen-year-old girl back then, because of the culture, you had to wait for somebody to come and ask. And sometimes it was:

Oh my God! Look at what's coming to ask me!

In those days, even though females had to wait for males to come to them, I would imagine the females could tell you the way they "got him." But as a male, it's very difficult and frustrating to imagine that one would have to sit and wait.

I think where it was blown for the male was prepuberty, because in prepuberty little girls wanted to be friends. And because of the animal-gland secretions, without the opening up of the puberty, males could only think of aggressive behavior in terms of a chase, but not to chase to capture — to actually chase away. The poor female was left confused, because boys were knocking them down, knocking their books out of their hands. There were even these strange tales of having their braids being dipped in the inkwell of the desk of the boy sitting behind them. And this was supposed to be funny.

But the boys had this aggression, to chase, to tease the female, leaving the female confused and saying that these boys are mean, and asking, "Why?" And I believe that there are grown women of whatever age who have scars still. Little scars, or maybe good-sized ones, on their knees and elbows, from some stupid boys, age five or six or seven, flying through the air like they'd turned themselves into some kind of human heat-seeking missiles. And I'm sure that some of these grown women, to this day, worry when they sit in a theater, that some male behind them is going to dip their hair in an inkwell and leap up and jump on their head.

I still remember, at the dance, girls on one side, boys on the other. The music on the 78 record — and it wasn't a diamond needle; this was just a plain old needle — blasting away, and these twelve-, thirteen-year-olds just standing there, afraid to make the long walk across the floor to the other side.

One of the most interesting aspects of human behavior is that they can stand there, I would imagine until they die, if the first person does not make that move. I don't know what goes on in other cultures, but in ours, each age-group, whatever group you're plumped with, at some point, before you ever get to dancing or whatever, you have to go through this awkward stage.

Things may have changed by now, but I just remember the auditorium, or gymnasium, and the girls are on one side and the boys are on the other, and they stand across from each other, like there's some giant moat. No alligators, no snakes, no electric wires, no quicksand, but to get from one side of the moat to the other was very scary. I think that each generation had to have someone who made the walk first. And that was the freeing moment. Otherwise, there wouldn't be a next generation. That walk, in itself, was the bravest move.

There we were, boys on one side and girls on the other, like human chess pieces. Everybody knows that in chess, the first move is very important. And the second move too. Plus, you have to think several moves ahead or you can get checkmated. The problem was, here were a bunch of fifteen-year-olds who couldn't even think one move ahead. We're all lined up, on the chessboard, as I said, with the girls on one side—who are talking with each other—and the boys on the other side. Everybody is thinking how to be cool, but even though we know we're supposed to go over there, we just can't go.

Now, this was in my day. Today, I don't know what

you do. You come in dancing or whatever. But back then, you stand there and the girls are there and the boys are supposed to do something. Finally it's a long enough wait that it becomes kind of silly.

Actually nobody stands back and says:

All right, are we men or not? Let's go get 'em.

But there is that one person, and I don't remember who it was, but that fellow, that brave fellow who went across and freed us. And then we all walked across and asked a girl to dance.

There's always a girl in one's life who will disappear but the story remains. That one, for me, was Bernadette Johnson. As I've said, Bernadette was fine. Everybody said it, all the fellows I was with, all the guys who were my buddies.

Bernadette was fine.

But she also was a wonderful person. Because as fine as she was, she did not "ig" you.

What is "ig"?

It's a word from my time that I will define for you.

You know how people say somebody "dissed" them? And you know what "dis" is short for: "disrespect." So "ig" is short for "ignore." As in, "She igged you." Which means she ignored you.

Bernadette would not "ig" you, even though she was fine. Even if you looked like Rondo Hatton, the actor in horror films who was nicknamed "the Creeper." He never talked, and he had that jaw and that long face and big hands and big feet. Really, he was a horrible-looking guy. They used him as a horror figure in movies like *The Pearl of Death* and *House of Horrors.*

The point is, even if you looked like "the Creeper," Bernadette, if you spoke to her, would still say hello and make you feel like: *Gee whiz, she is fine, but she stopped to talk to me.*

When somebody had a party in the cellar, fifteen-, sixteen-year-olds had a party, with the parents upstairs, you just felt wonderful. There was fresh whitewash on the walls. And you could never really fully stand up if you were six foot one.

There was always punch on the table, alcohol-free punch. And the 78s were like two minutes long, so that if the song was slow, you could dance close. And I'm talking about dancing cheek to cheek for two minutes, which gave you enough time to put in a couple of smooth moves. But then the record was over and you had to walk the girl back to where she was before, and you went back to where the boys were. As you got older, you stopped talking about what happened. You just came back and that was your secret.

But even then, at these parties in the basement, Berna-dette wouldn't reject you. She just made you feel wonder-ful. In those days, the style of the skirt was very tight, tight around the waist, above the hip, and then it came tight around the side, went down, and then flared out down to some very thin, light lace socks and black flat shoes. Girls' blouses had sort of that Spanish flair, and it was almost off the shoulder, and short-sleeved, slightly puffy, usually white, and it looked like a string or, I don't know, a strip of elastic held things together. Everything was covered and so you had to look for it, which I still think is a lot of fun. As opposed to today, where some of the girls walking around make you wonder: *Well, what's left?*

But there were a few girls who did reject. They didn't do it in a bad way. When you asked them to dance they would say:

No, not right now.

Obviously the girl was waiting for somebody else, and now you're standing there with nowhere to go. I do remember once I asked two, three girls in a row, but got rejected and just went back to where the fellows were.

But I don't remember Bernadette turning anybody down. That's how nice she was. She danced every dance. She spoke to everyone. In other words, she was sort of, if you wanted to define her, a teenage angel. Nobody ever said anything bad about her. Even the girls all knew that she was fine.

Bernadette didn't have an ugly girlfriend. She had sisters. Four sisters, all of them fine. Bernadette Johnson. She was nice. She was hip.

She was fine.

Buzzy Reed told Ron Brown that Cleofus Smith said

Bernadette dug (loved) Miles Davis records. I said, "What?"

So I went up to her—the thing about Miles Davis records armed me and made me brave. Ordinarily, I'd be scared to death to talk to Bernadette too much. But that day I went up to her.

I said, "Bernadette, I understand that you're digging Miles Davis."

She said, "I love Miles Davis, William."

I said, "Well, I happen to have every one of the newest Miles Davis LPs ever made."

She said, "Oh my goodness."

I said, "Would you like to listen to the ones I have?"

She said, "I would love to, William."

I didn't hear anything else after that. I just started to walk away. I was so happy, I was just going.

She said, "William?"

I said, "Yes?"

She said, "When?"

I said, "What?"

She said, "When are you going to play your records for me?"

I said, "When?"

She said, "That's what I'm asking you."

I started to feel stupid. You know, that's one thing that'll climb all over you, when you know you're stupid. And you're in love.

I said, "Friday."

She said, "Where?"

I said, "I'll come to your house."

She said, "Do you know where I live?"

I said, "No."

She said, "Well, then, let me give you my address."

After I got her address, I walked away. I was so in love; I was so happy. Bernadette Johnson. She gave me her address. But there was one problem.

I did not have one Miles Davis record.

But Joe Barnett did. So I went to my man, Joe. My friend, Joe Barnett. You see, that's the meaning of a friend. Your child can't be your friend. Your child's got nothin' you can borrow. Joe Barnett loaned me four of the latest Miles Davis LPs. Only thing I had to do was spill ink. He had a stamp that said, "Property of Joe Barnett." So I spilled ink on it.

Friday finally came. I bathed three times. We didn't have a shower, just a bathtub. Bathed three times because . . .

Gonna see Bernadette Johnson!

And after the third bath, I remembered that my father, who was in the navy and had been all around the world, brought home a bottle of Canoe cologne. So I filled the tub with about a foot of water, climbed in, and poured the whole bottle of Canoe—it was unopened, never been used—in the water. Emptied that bottle out. As I sat in the tub being marinated (burned, actually, or sautéed) the Canoe cleared up my athlete's feet and I discovered parts of my body that I hadn't thought about. A normal person would have gotten out of the tub, but I could think only of how wonderful I would smell for the lovely Bernadette.

Gonna see Bernadette Johnson!

Then I filled the empty Canoe bottle with water and put it back on the shelf in case some grown-up noticed and asked, "What happened to the Canoe?"

"Well, it's so old, it just lost its fragrance."

As I started to get dressed, I noticed that I was coughing.

What's wrong? Why am I coughing?

And then I realized the Canoe was cutting off my breathing. Eyes running, coughing, the more clothes I put on, the more air would come up into my face and I couldn't get away from the smell. I was upstairs in my bedroom. My mother was in the kitchen.

She said, "What is that up there? What are you doing up there?"

I said, "Nothing, Mother."

She said, "What's wrong with your voice?"

So I came down the steps, dressed, and I picked up the LPs. Even though my mother was way back in the kitchen . . .

She said, "What have you got on?"

I said, "Uh, I don't know. It's a new soap."

As I left the house, I could hear my mother opening the windows.

When you're fifteen years old, you've got two things going for you: stupidity and hope. Bernadette's house was a block and a half from our house, and I'm hoping this smell will be gone by the time I get to her house. Because it was strong. Really strong. Like ewwww strong.

I got to her house, went up these wooden steps to the porch, and pulled open the aluminum screen door. Just doing that, the air came back at me, and oh, the smell!

I rang the doorbell. When she opened the door it sucked the Canoe fumes off of me. Tears formed in her eyes and she said, "Oh, come on in right away."

As I went past her, she looked outside, wrinkled her nose, then turned to her mother. I heard her mother say, "No, it's him."

Meaning it was me who smelled.

Bernadette looked fine. But that smell was in the way of everything. When I went to say hello to Bernadette's mother, she stood back and said, "Just stay where you are, son. It's very nice to meet you."

Bernadette's father said, "Take care of yourself."

And he left. He just left.

Then the mother said something to Bernadette about how she knows what time to say good night and then went upstairs.

Bernadette was so nice. She smiled. And she just looked so fine. But it was hot in the house and oh God, the heat, the Canoe, the heat, the perfume. Oh God! The smell just kept coming and coming. Bernadette was sitting there. She excused herself and when she came back she had a fan. It was one of those fans from a funeral parlor, So-and-So's Funeral Parlor. You know, the ones you get in church. I don't know why funeral parlors do that—make a fan telling you, you gonna die. You're fanning the thing and it's telling you you're going to die.

So we're sitting there on the couch and she's just fanning herself.

So I said, "I have the LPs."

She said, "Oh, let me help you."

I said, "No, I'll do it."

She said, "Good."

I think she said that because of the fact that I was about to move away from her. So I went over to the console, which I knew how to work because Joe Barnett had one. I turned it on, pulled the Miles Davis LPs out, put four of them up on the spindle, brought the holder back over to keep the four records in place, turned the speed to 33 1/3, and pushed the controls to "play." The arm with the diamond needle (and a quarter Scotch-taped to the top) came up and did a searching move to set itself for the size of the 33 1/3 record, then dropped down, and the music started. I said, "Yeah."

When I turned around, Bernadette was sitting on the sofa. Now, she could have sat in the armchair, but she sat on the sofa. I'm not thinking about "getting some." I'm in love with Bernadette Johnson. I want to marry her. I will get a job, I will buy her a house, and we will have two cars. And I'm saving myself for her.

I sat down. She had her left hand on the cushion, so accidentally, my hand went down, and my little finger went on top of her little finger. And then she took her little finger and put it on top of three of my other fingers. I don't know how it happened, but all of a sudden, I heard myself say, "Oh yeah." I was so happy. I don't know where it came from, just "Oh yeah." Then I took her hand, asking permission first, and turned, and she was looking at me and she was smiling and Miles Davis was playing away.

Then I noticed her father leaning on the opening leading to the dining room. He's got a revolver, with the cylinder open. And he's got a stick with cotton, which he is using to clean the chambers. He looked at me and he said, "You live about a block and a half away, left-hand side of the street?"

I said, "Yes, sir."

He said, "You got twin brick posts and an iron gate leading to your steps and the porch?"

I said, "Yes, sir."

He looked at me and nodded a "yes" and said, "I just want to know where to come."

He slapped the gun so that the cylinder went back in and made a noise. *Click!* And then he turned and went into the dining room.

I said, "Bernadette, I have an awful lot of homework to do."

She said, "So soon? It's Friday."

I said, "And a good time to leave."

I left so fast I forgot to take the albums. I called Joe Barnett and told him where to go and pick them up, and the next day Joe went over to get his LPs.

Four years later, he and Bernadette were married. I was one of the groomsmen at their wedding. Bernadette's father came up to me and said, "I just want you to know something. I didn't think anything was wrong with you except you just didn't smell right. I just kept saying to myself, 'I gotta live with a son-in-law smelling like this for the rest of my life? I don't think so.'" Then he gave me a great handshake and said, "However, you do smell a lot better. Thank God."

MESSAGE TO THE GROOM

Think about having *your* mother (not *her* father) escort your bride down the aisle. When you turn around and watch them approach, you will be able to see your whole life coming at you. Your mother, that dear, lovely woman who saved everything while you were growing up—trophies, school papers, drawings, everything you ever did—walking with the woman who, as time goes by, will throw all these things out.

THE MORPHAMIZATION OF
PEANUT ARMHOUSE

I was in my forties at the time, performing at Harrah's in Atlantic City. After the show, my agent came in the dressing room and asked me, "Do you know anybody named M.C.?"

"No."

"Well, he says he knows you from your old neighborhood in the projects."

"M.C.? Are those his initials?"

"I don't know."

To me, "M.C." could mean the master of ceremonies at a show. Was this someone who emceed one of my shows?

"Go back out and ask him what M.C. stands for."

A few minutes later, my agent returned: "He said it doesn't stand for anything. M.C. That's his whole name."

And then the light went on. *Em*cee! I remember Emcee! And I said, "Bring him back."

In walks a guy in his forties whom I hadn't seen for more than thirty years—the last time I saw him he was eight. Tonight he's wearing a sports coat and a tie, with a hat like Humphrey Bogart wore, a fedora or whatever it's called. He has a mustache now, and a goatee. But somewhere in there I could see Emcee. And he's got his wife with him, whom he introduced as "my wife." Nothing more. She's a very handsome woman, all dressed up, hair done, makeup, everything perfect. She was just smiling, happy to be there.

Emcee, I find out, works at the post office in Philadelphia, and his wife has a job at Grant's Awnings on Chelten Avenue. They tell me they have three children.

We then began reminiscing. His wife sat there with a wife smile, probably not caring about these stories. But I could see that she was thinking: *Yes, my husband really does know Bill Cosby.*

"Remember that day when I was at bat," Emcee said at one point, "and I hit the ball and it bounced off Pedro's hand?"

I do remember because I was the pitcher when Pedro made the error that put Emcee on first base. The ball went off Pedro's glove, ran up his arm and across his shoulder, and then hit him in the left side of his head, causing a sharp ringing. After that, he didn't care where the ball was—he just kept opening and closing his mouth—because he couldn't hear for a while.

"Oh yes," I said. "And then Peanut Armhouse picked up the bat and..."

My voice trailed off because just thinking about that day gave me chills. I have seen a lot of things in my life. A lot of things. But I have never, to this day, seen anything like the morphamization of Peanut Armhouse. And no one who was there will ever forget it.

I grew up on Parrish Place in the Richard Allen projects in Philadelphia. The people who were allowed in these housing projects were husbands and wives. Mothers living with fathers, fathers who were doing something, mothers who were doing something, sometimes as a domestic, so they could get cash as quietly as possible and keep it under the table—if there even was a table. And people were in the projects on a promissory note that they would work to build themselves up and move out, which I must say, all the guys I knew, their parents actually did that. Many of the guys went on to a better life. Like Ron Davenport, who graduated from college and became the dean of the University of Pittsburgh law school.

There was an area where we played softball, which was around back and was called "Around Back" because it was...around back. Around the back of a row of housing-project-type apartments that started at the end of Ninth Street, near the Ninth Street Bridge. Parallel to these buildings was another row of apartments. The backs of these two apartment buildings formed a large rectangular area between them: "Around Back." I think when they built the projects, somebody said, *Let's create a field where kids can play.*

The area we played on wasn't loose gravel, but it was very rough, so the ball didn't last long. The surface was like what you see on roads with the tar and the white specks. I later found out that the specks were something called pea stone. They would take hot tar and then pour pea stone on top of it, and then a steamroller weighing twenty tons and operated by a professional steamroller operator, who at the time was making six dollars an hour, mashed the pea stone into the tar.

I will now give you a description of the surface that we played on "Around Back" in the same manner a waiter at a gourmet restaurant would tell you about what's on the menu.

The chef has taken hot tar from the mountains of Ethiopia and added decorative, six-millimeter golden pea shingle with block edging, which has been carefully crafted from the purest Indian sandstone.

We just called it "the ground."

After the tar dries, it stays sort of gray and it's more or less smooth but still rough on skin that travels over it at six miles an hour. When you're traveling six miles an hour, you come up skinned. Strawberry comes to mind.

Streaks and scrapes of brown and white and red soon to become a long scab.

When I was at Central High School I made the football team. The freshman practice field was in a park. Plenty of grass and trees. At the first practice a guy threw a ball to me. I bent over while running, but it was out of my reach even running bent over with my arms extended.

The coach yelled at me, "You *dive* for those!"

I can't say he challenged my manhood—I was just a kid—but he made it sound like I was afraid to dive.

"Dive for that ball, son! *Dive!*"

What? Dive? I never dove for anything in my life. I don't even know what it's like to dive. When you're brought up playing on tar and pea stone, which is unforgiving, there is no diving. Dirt and grass, sure, you can dive. But we didn't have dirt and grass. We had tar and pea stone and broken glass. There was no diving. No sliding into second base or third base. Certainly no headfirst into first. *You did not slide.*

When you played football, you didn't dive either, because it was not dirt—it was tar and pea stone. This kind of surface is not for diving to catch a pass. You just let it go and it was understood. Coming from a surface of tar and pea stone, there are no arms stretched out in the air parallel to the ground to catch a newspaper rolled up with rubber bands for a gain of seven yards. Dive?

I don't think so.

We didn't have real bases when we played softball. We drew the bases with crayons or colored chalk—first base, second base, third, and home. We drew home plate so that the batter's back was parallel to the first row of apartments, and right field was the second parallel row. There was a drain about twenty feet to the right of second base, a grated drain three feet by three feet. Don't step on that, because the front part of your Cat's Paw rubber sole might get caught under one of the bars and you will have it pulled off and run around with a flapping sole.

At some point they put in monkey bars, the famous monkey bars, and they sat somewhere out in center field behind second base, maybe thirty feet past second base. Before the monkey bars nobody got hurt. Children fell, were cut by glass and things like that, but they were minor injuries that a Band-Aid could cover. No stitches. Then they put in monkey bars, this steel structure, and kids wound up in the hospital. I think someone who did not like children invented the monkey bars and said, *Look, this will get rid of a lot of them.*

There was a fence on Ninth Street that ends the block. (Yes, we had fences too in those days.) And behind that fence was the famous Fat Albert Ninth Street Bridge. A ball hit over that fence was a home run. There was also an area that was sandy dirt, and obviously this was for kids to draw circles and shoot marbles or maybe somebody said they could play and make sand castles or mud castles or something.

We were very serious when we played softball. Especially when we pitched. We'd throw the ball as fast as we could. It wasn't a looping throw six feet in the air, which is second only to T-ball placement, where you hit a ball off a stationary tee. No, what we threw was a hard pitch — with spin.

Anyway, we were in the middle of a softball game when Peanut Armhouse's mother came, and she stood in the center of the sandy dirt place. She had an apron on. (Most of the mothers had aprons.) And she called Peanut, the way parents called in those days, using vowels because vowels carried farther than consonants.

"Peeee-nut!"

She hit hard on the *p* and stretched out the *e*. The "nut" was very short. You could hardly hear the "nut." But everybody knew she was calling Peanut. It was the sound.

One of the most difficult names for parents who hadn't planned ahead was Ronald. You can't get off a loud Ronald. Everything dies — Raaaaan-aaaald. That's about as close as you can get. You can't hit an *a* as high as an *e* or an *i*. The name Ronald kind of dies, so you get the nickname Ronnie.

Bobby Wiggins' mother could whistle. She'd put two fingers in her mouth, and man, that sound shrilled. Everybody knew that was Bobby Wiggins' call. Bobby Wiggins' mother would whistle from the apartment; she never came down. She just opened the window and whistled. And Bobby never said anything; he always left without a word. He didn't even say, "Got to go." He just ran and went down through the clothes yard.

The clothes yard was an area about fifty-five feet by sixty feet, where every Monday people in Apartments B and C and higher letters took their wash and, because there were no clothes dryers, hung their clothes out to be dried by the sun on the clothesline in the clothes yard (which says something about honesty in those days). They used wooden clothespins only. No clamps.

People in an A apartment didn't have to go to the clothes yard because all A apartments had a backyard with grass where they hung their clothes out. Although it wasn't big enough to dive for anything, it was just large enough so that there was a point in time when we grew tomatoes and collard greens, but that turned out to be mostly for the enjoyment of the uninvited bugs.

We lived at 919, Apartment A, Parrish Place. So we didn't have to go to the clothes yard. To get to my house from Tenth Street—where the number 23 trolley ran going south—you got off the trolley car, waited for it to pass, crossed Tenth Street, went to the right into the complex onto Hutchinson Place, which is perpendicular to Parrish Place, where I lived. When we first moved there, I thought that the sound of the green wooden trolley would keep me awake. But it never did.

After crossing Tenth Street, you walked past the Trash House, which was to the right, the place where, obviously, we put the trash — that's why it's called the Trash House. To the left was the Garbage House, which was attached to our building and was called the Garbage House for the same reason: People put garbage in the Garbage House. Sometimes people got lazy and put the trash in the Garbage House. But they never caught anybody doing it.

Even if you were unsighted, you could tell the Garbage House from the Trash House because the Garbage House had a buzzing hum from the eighteen billion flies having an indoor, trash-can buffet. Flies of all species: metallic green and blue colors, dangerous looking. Flies with attitudes. They just landed on you and stayed there and dared you to hit them. That's okay, though. I paid them back in October when they were slow. I didn't even have to be fast. Just a nice little gentle tap. Then I'd put them outside.

The Trash House and Garbage House were about ten feet high. They were brick, had windows, and had grass around them. There was grass everywhere in those days (except "Around Back," which was tar and pea stone). There were trees, but they were only as wide as my wrist, as the wrist of an eight-year-old boy. Following the path of the fence, you arrived at my apartment — 919-A Parrish Place.

By the way, this description is no longer any good, so do not look for what I've been describing. Do not Wikipedia it or Google it or anything. And please do not go on any social network searching for a picture of this. It isn't there anymore, because like anything in anybody's life, if you live long enough, you will eventually say, "Wait a minute! It used to be here but they tore it all down."

As you get older, even if you're thirty now, in another thirty years you're going to be telling somebody, "This used to be Philadelphia, but it isn't any longer because now it's Elmwood."

So, back then, when you got to 919-A Parrish Place, it was one step up to a big maroon door with — *excuse me!* — *real* glass windows. And then another step after you pulled the maroon door open using brass knobs, no key needed, which put you in the hallway. There was a bell in the center that went *kriiing* when you turned the handle.

Apartment A was on the first floor. Apartments B and C were on the second floor. To the left, on the wall, were three mailboxes: A, B, and C.

The only time I ever got mail was when I was twelve

and I believed a Charles Atlas ad. I was skinny, and even though I had never been on the beach and even though nobody had ever kicked sand in my face, I liked his body and I wanted one just like it. And it said "free."

So I sent away and I thought I was going to get all these dumbbells and everything. But then a letter came back from Charles Atlas and it said something about sending them some money first. I don't remember how much; I just know it scared me. I mean, it *really* scared me when that letter came and they were asking for money. I am not lying. It's the absolute truth. I never, ever had to think about money outside of going to the store or shining shoes on the corner. I had never dealt with the huge corporate powers of the world. When they wrote that letter to me, my first-ever piece of mail, and said to me they wanted some money, I couldn't believe it. *The ad said "free"!* It was the first time I ever experienced a free that was not free. And this was before credit cards and identity theft. Although I had no identity to steal.

Besides the letter asking for money, there were these papers that I had to sign. I was scared because they wanted money and I really didn't know how to answer them. So I wrote them back:

Dear Mr. Atlas: This is William's mother. My son is crazy so please leave him alone.

And they did.

To this day, I have never paid any attention to any magazines offering anything. I said then, at the age of twelve, from now on, the word "free"—I'm not going for it.

Next door to us, at 917-A Parrish Place, was an elderly woman who was "of the church," and everybody called her Mother Harold. They called her Mother Harold because of her religion, which was...I don't know. Anyway, she chased the children for skateboarding in front of her house or riding a bike fast or loud talking. She was always chasing anyone ten years or younger. So we put "old" in front of her name and we called her "Old Mother Harold."

When you're children, "old" is a problem. Old people always telling you something. I just thought that I was put on this earth so old people could call me over for something. Or send me to the store for something.

All of us seven-, eight-, nine-, ten-year-olds thought Old Mother Harold had nothing better to do than sit in her house, perhaps with the door of the apartment open so she could get out faster, waiting to chase us. She never touched anybody. Even if you fell, she would just come out there and stand over you and say:

I told you about skating in front of this house.

You would get up and grab your wooden skateboard, walk away, then put it down and skate hard to make noise. But you never yelled at her. You never yelled out, "Old Mother Harold!"

Unless you were far away.

Just to let you know, these were not your modern skateboards. They were made from roller skates, street roller skates, which had clamps that went into the front sole of your shoe. You'd tighten the clamps with a skate key, but this was not good for your shoes because it pulled on your sole and then you'd see your toes coming out. So you'd get a piece of wood, say, three feet long. Then you'd take the piece of rubber out of the front of the skates—which would let the wheels move left and right. Next, you clamped the skate to the wood, plus you nailed the skate down. And you had a skateboard.

Old Mother Harold wore white all the time. Even her stockings were white and her shoes were white. Her hair was natural and platted, neatly, though, but never pressed or straightened.

Since Old Mother Harold's apartment was an A apartment on the first floor, you could look in through her front window. It seemed she never had any lights on that anybody could see, and when she did turn on lights, they were blue, so it was always dark in her apartment.

On Halloween, Old Mother Harold's door was the one door you didn't knock on. You never even went in the hall to go upstairs to the B and C apartments and beg. (We called it begging—other people called it trick or treat.) Most of us dressed up with pillowcases—we didn't have any money for masks — and we put a little lipstick on and went around with a brown paper bag.

You just had a feeling, man, if you rang that doorbell and Old Mother Harold came to the door, she might be bigger than she really is and she would get *you* for Halloween! Standing there about seven feet tall with hands bigger than a bushel basket to scoop you up. You would never come out of that hallway alive! All people would find would be a little pillowcase that you had used for a cape. And a piece of cardboard pumpkin that you brought home from school because the next day the school wouldn't need Halloween stuff.

Back to the softball game and the morphamization of Peanut Armhouse.

I was the pitcher. While I waited for the next batter to come to the plate, Peanut's mother called him a second time:

"Peeee-nut!"

And this wasn't just anybody calling Peanut; it was a *mother*.

Usually it was the mother who, besides working, would fix you breakfast and send you off to school. If she didn't work, you walked home on your break and your mother made you lunch. Then when you got out of school at three o'clock, you went back home and your mother had a snack waiting for you. Then she cooked dinner. There was no fast food. She cooked. Mothers had quite a job to do.

I went to Mary Channing Wister Elementary School. I just walked from my house straight down to Ninth Street — underneath the famous Fat Albert Ninth Street Bridge — and then up to Eighth and Parrish. After school I'd walk back home, put my books down — no studying here. No homework either.

"Any homework?" my mother would ask.

My reply: "No homework."

"I thought you had homework."

"Already did it."

And then, *bam!* I'd change from my school clothes to my play clothes and head "Around Back."

Somewhere around four, everybody was out. I don't know where the bat came from; I never had a bat of my own. I never had a glove of my own either. And I don't know where the softball came from, but it didn't come from my apartment because my apartment had no money. There was no money for contributing to any purchase of a softball, to any purchase of an orange soda. Nothing. The money was just not there. Therefore, I do not remember clearly how anything, especially a brand-new softball, wound up "Around Back." I guess some kid's father bought it. A quality softball in those days might have cost seventy-five cents. So somebody's father bought a ball. It didn't come from the people in the projects; it was the father of one of the boys who lived somewhere else.

Bobby Stevenson really hit the ball hard. So did Hubert McClinton, who was the first one to go into the service. When he came back from basic training wearing a uniform, Hubert got us together and taught us all to march. Don't forget, we were little kids, eight, nine years old. And he was wearing a uniform. So there we were, lined up and marching, really for no reason. After a while nobody showed up for Hubert's marches.

Bobby and Hubert were the only people who ever knocked the ball onto the Ninth Street Bridge, which was quite a wallop, and that was another reason the ball didn't last long. First the stitches would come apart and pretty soon you're hitting an egg with dirt and stuff falling out of it. Then the cover would come off and then there was all this string. Those were the good balls. The bad balls looked good in the beginning but didn't even last long enough for the cover to come off. They were like piñatas. They just exploded.

So the cover would come off and, once again, I had no money for a new ball and neither did anybody else. So somebody would stop the game, and one of the older guys—by older I mean somebody around age eleven—would say:

Okay, we've got to get some tape.

And somebody, I don't remember who, somebody

went and came back with black tape, electrical tape, and Bobby Stevenson said: *This is not good tape.* And it wasn't. The black electrical tape, even though we wrapped it around the ball really well, picked up glass and pebbles. Somebody would hit a ground ball and it would bounce, bounce, bounce, and you'd catch it — we played with bare hands; I don't remember too many guys with gloves—and you wound up with that ball spinning and all that stuff it had picked up went around in your hands. Pebbles, pieces of glass, cutting into your hands. Plus, the tape was sticky and it wasn't fun to play with it.

A much better tape—we're talking quality—was the white Red Cross tape from the pharmacy. The white Red Cross tape was the best because it wasn't sticky and it didn't pick up the glass, the stones, the pebbles. Not only was it not sticky; it was white. Which was also the color of the cover of the ball. And we played with that sometimes. Of course, after a while, the tape would start to go and you'd have to retape it.

"Peeee-nut!"

This particular day, the day Peanut Armhouse's mother called him to come home, it was the electrician's tape. I was the pitcher. And Emcee had just been to bat and hit a single. Actually, it wasn't a single. Pedro was playing third base and the ball bounced off his hand, so it was Pedro's error that put Emcee on first base. We called him Pee-dro because to us "pe" was pronounced "pee." His father was really not happy with this and kept correcting people. I think he even went around to people's houses and said:

My son's first name is pronounced Pay-dro.

But even though his father wanted it "Paydro,"

49

Pedro did answer to "Pee-dro." Anyway, Emcee had just been at bat. He dropped the bat and ran to first.

Now, in softball, you cannot steal. You had to stand on the base. Or you could move your foot off the base a little, but you couldn't steal. You could take off running only after the ball was released from the pitcher's hand. And that's because, I guess, the bases were very close together.

So Emcee was on first. I had the ball, ready for the next batter. And Peanut's mother was still standing in the sandy dirt area.

"Peee-nut! Dinner is ready!"

Like I said before, mothers cooked. You could smell dinners — I mean, all of these aromas mixed together were just something wonderful — but the smell was never enough to make you so hungry that you wanted to go home and leave the "game." The "game" was *that* powerful.

Now, Peanut grabs the bat. We had only one bat. Everybody had to bat with the same bat, and it had broken, but not in half or anything. It had a nail driven through it to keep the two pieces together, so you had to be careful where you held it because if you held it around the back of the nail, you could really put a hole in your hand and draw blood.

Peanut's mother is standing there with that apron

on. And Peanut has the bat. But that's okay; I have the ball. And there's no way I'm throwing it to Peanut.

Because my mother knows Peanut's mother.

And Peanut's mother calls out:

"Put the bat down, Peanut."

"But, Momma," Peanut yells back, "I haven't had a bat yet! I just want to bat and I will be right there!"

"I don't care how many bats you have coming. Dinner is ready!"

"But, *Momma*—"

"Peanut! I am not cooking for my health!"

"Please, Momma!"

"What did I just say?"

"But, Momma—"

"Come off that field now!"

But instead of running off the field, Peanut raises the bat and calls out to me:

"Come on, man, throw the ball! Throw me the ball!"

After he said that, I heard the rising sound of his mother's voice:

"Peee-nut! I am not fooling with you!"

Pit Bull McCoy is the catcher. And Pit Bull looks at me with fear on his face.

Because Pit Bull's mother knows Peanut's mother.

"Peee-nut!"

Peanut then sort of morphs into a boy who is lost. I

think this is the first time I ever saw — I had heard about it, but I had actually never seen with my eyes — somebody who had gone crazy. Completely crazy. I had never witnessed a boy who had lost his mind. But Peanut had lost his mind. Everybody could see it.

Peanut waves his hand at me:

"Come on, man! Throw me the ball!"

And when I don't throw him the ball, Peanut walks toward me with the bat in his hand.

Now every kid on that field is focused on Peanut; every kid has the same expression. Our jaws just dropped. There's no frown on anybody's forehead. It's just a look of stunned boys, eight, nine years old, looking at a morphed boy. I mean, we're all seeing the same thing: a morphed boy.

I set the ball down on the ground.

Because my mother knows Peanut's mother.

I'm not about to have Peanut's mother come to my mother and say:

I told Peanut to come off the field. And your *son threw the ball to him.*

So Peanut walks out. I had put the ball down in front of me on the mound, and I just stand there looking at him. We are all looking at him. Nobody talked. Just looked. Peanut walks out nervously, morphing even more. No foam around the mouth or anything, just an insane determination to destroy himself.

Peanut bends down, picks up the ball, then walks back to home plate. And Peanut's mother yells:

"Peee-nut! Put the bat down!"

But it was too late. Peanut had morphed too far to hear his mother.

Somehow we all knew that this was not a good experience. I don't remember feeling anything—I think I was numb—but I do remember watching a performance of something no one had ever seen. I think our dopamine level was off the scale. This was not a *fight, fight, fight* kind of dopamine. This was a stunned spike in dopamine. We were all stunned. Unbelievably stunned. We had all become statues.

So Peanut goes back to home plate. He tosses the ball into the air, takes a big swing, and hits the ball. It wasn't even a good hit. As a matter of fact, it was rather pitiful.

The ball rolls toward Skeets. Skeets doesn't move. The ball rolls past Skeets. Skeets could have picked it up and thrown to first and Peanut would have been out. But he didn't.

Because Skeets' mother knew Peanut's mother.

You see, none of us wanted to be an accomplice or even an accessory to the fact. An accessory to the mor-phamization of Peanut Armhouse. Some of us could have said, "Come on, man, go on home." Like you tell a drunk. But we didn't.

We were statues. Still no movement of blood. And here's this ball rolling at the rate of about four miles an hour. I use that because a lot of walkers will know that speed. Or, let's say, the speed of a golfer's fifty-foot putt.

Peanut drops the bat. Then, with clenched fists, begins to announce as Byron Saam would at a Philadel-phia Phillies game:

"Peee-nut Armhouse has just hit a blazing, scorch-ing ground ball past Skeets Washington."

Peanut starts running, announcing his every move.

"Peanut is headed to first."

And the ball is still rolling. It goes into where the monkey bars are and it's bouncing like a pinball in a pin-ball machine. There's Israel Johnson, who is playing center field. He's standing there at the monkey bars where the ball is bouncing around. Suddenly, the ball bounces up. Israel jumps like a scared cat so the ball doesn't touch him. He jumped like I haven't seen anybody jump before. He did not want to become an accessory.

Because Israel Johnson's mother knows Peanut's mother.

Meanwhile, Peanut is still announcing.

"Peanut steps on first base!"

Emcee is standing on first base watching Peanut run past him. Nobody says a thing.

"Peanut rounds first!"

Emcee stays on first, so obviously Peanut is out. But Peanut keeps on announcing.

"Peanut is now rounding second...Peanut tags second...Peanut is now in the groove and running at a nice pace...Peanut is rounding third, he tags third... Peanut is on his way home for an inside-the-box home run!"

Peanut jumps into the air and lands, ladies and gentlemen, with both feet on home plate. Stomps on home plate! Thrusts his arms in the air.

"A home run for Peanut Armhouse, greatest hitter in the world!"

And then Peanut runs toward where his mother was standing.

But Peanut's mother is not where she was. She is

gone. We were still statues as we watched Peanut disappear into his house.

And we never saw

Peanut

Glanville

Roosevelt

Armhouse

again.

• • •

There were inquiries. A social worker came around look-ing for Peanut. A census taker asked questions. I don't really think he was a census taker, just an investigator pretending to be a census taker. The FBI would stop by once in a while. People complied, they talked, but I don't remember anybody ever saying that there was ever, in fact, anyone by the name of Peanut Armhouse. His sister Tomasina, cute with dimples, never spoke of her brother.

It was exactly a year later and I believe the time was exactly the same. We were "Around Back" playing soft-ball. It was the fifth inning, and we were leading 55 to 48. I was pitching. Bobby Stevenson was on second. Freddy was in center field. Emcee was at bat again. Seafus McNeely had replaced Pedro at third base. Because Pedro was always making errors—like when he let Emcee reach first base the day Peanut Armhouse morphed—we moved him to right field, where nobody ever hits any-thing. Plus, it was Seafus' ball and he wanted to play third base or else he would take his ball and go home.

Seafus' ball was brand-new, and even though we had scored fifty-five runs, it was still hard and still had a cover on it. And that ball went fast. So when Emcee hit the ball, it took off. A line drive right at Seafus. And it was a sight to behold: Seafus clapped his hands—his gloved hand and the other hand—like a person trying to catch a ball in midair. But the clap was too late. So first you heard a clap

and then you heard *thwop!* Which was the sound of the ball striking Seafus dead center on his forehead. You see, Seafus' timing was awful because he really can't play. And, as I said, the only reason he's playing is because it's his ball.

Since Seafus was not a well-liked person, this was, for all of us, one of the great moments that, even as old men, we remember. That Seafus McNeely got hit by a line drive. It wasn't really a scorching line drive, maybe

two miles an hour faster than a pop fly. *Clap!* Then...
thwop! The sound of the ball, his own ball, hitting him
square in the middle of his forehead. So karma was there
even back in those days.

When Seafus was hit in the forehead, he immediately
fell on top of the ball. I ran to him, turned him over,
grabbed the ball, then faked throwing to second in
order to make Emcee stop at first.

We left Seafus on the ground, out cold. Which was a
better position for Seafus. That way the left fielder could
see what was going on. There was no obstruction. (If
you ever meet a grown man around seventy-three years
old as of this writing, look carefully at his forehead. You
can still see the imprint of the stitches.)

All of a sudden, the most magnificent thing I had
ever witnessed in my nine years occurred. A black but-
terfly appeared over home plate — just fluttering it's
beautiful wings calmly to stay in the same position about
five feet high. Hubert McClinton, the catcher, saw it from
a crouched position. And then we heard it. It wasn't
loud, but we all heard it. It hovered there for a moment
over home plate, spread its wings like Ferko, then said:

Come on man! Throw me the ball!

As I sat there talking with Emcee, I think it may
have been the first actual disclosure that there ever was a
Peanut Armhouse.

"Come on man! Throw me the ball!" And as I heard myself say that to Emcee and his wife, I was searching way back, struggling to remember. *"Come on man…"*

Emcee turned to his wife: "You see, dear, I told you I wasn't making all that up."

She looked at him and I felt that she did believe him, and he smiled the biggest smile in the world.

They got up to leave. I stood and hugged him. "Emcee," I asked, "what's your real name?"

He smiled, a smaller smile, and said, "Just Emcee."

And then I hugged his wife, stepped back and asked, "Then what is your name?"

She said, "Mrs. Emcee," and she winked.

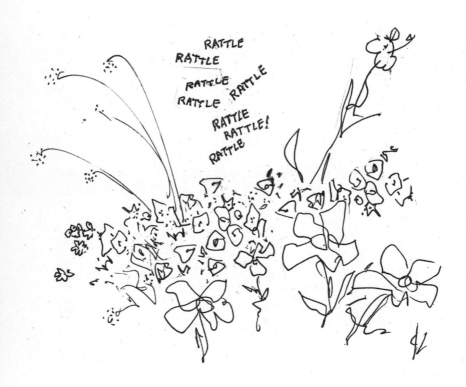

THE MISSING PAGES

I was raised a Christian and I was baptized and I believe. I sincerely believe. Why do I believe? Because any man or woman has to be a fool to say they don't believe. If you say you don't believe, something bad is going to happen, I believe. So I believe it's safer to say I believe than to not believe. And I believe you can have an out if you say, *I believe*. Not just *say* it, but really believe.

But if you *say* you believe, do they look at you on Judgment Day and ask: Do you *really* believe? Or do they say your belief doesn't count because you said so at the last minute because you got scared. You could say, *No, I wasn't scared. I said it out of fear. It says in the Bible: Fear the Lord your God.*

I do fear God. And I fear going to Hell or Purgatory. I have this picture of Hell, where there's a lot of laughing going on but nobody's having fun. And I know Purgatory when I see it. I've been on the Los Angeles Freeway when there's been a traffic jam for five hours and the temperature was a hundred and there were thunderstorms at ten-minute intervals.

Hell or Purgatory? What else you got? Turn over another card. Which is exactly why it's better to believe. So I *do* believe. And I have faith. But even though I realize that faith and fact are not always related, I need some help when it comes to Genesis.

For example, I own eight Bibles, all written in English. They were published at different times. One of them in 705. Another one was printed in 1709. And there's one that came over on the *Santa Maria*. They're all very old, but none are autographed.

One thing these Bibles have in common is the fact that I'm convinced there are missing pages. I don't know if the writers left things out or the editor cut things out or the publisher decided there wasn't enough space. I don't know. I just know that dealing with newspapers or magazines that interviewed me, when they left things out and I asked why, they said they didn't have enough space. When they don't tell the whole story, their excuse is they didn't have space. Even though it was their own newspaper, they chose not to clear up things because they didn't have the space. But what they really mean is: *We don't care what you said*. One time, when I demanded to know the reason something was left out of an interview, the writer implicated the editor and the editor blamed the publisher and the publisher offered up an indictment of the owner, who said it was all the accountant's fault because the accountant said, *We don't have enough paper.*

So when writers and editors and publishers and owners and accountants are involved, there's always something left out of the story. I call this "missing stuff." And I'm telling you, there is missing stuff in the Bible. Missing pages. And I don't know where these missing pages happen to be—maybe they're buried in Utah somewhere—but there are definitely missing pages. And I don't blame God for the jumping around in the story of his beginning; I blame the writers and editors. You see, every time you put God's word into human hands, it becomes messed up. Which is where the phrase "God only knows" comes from. After you read the Bible, it's very clear that God only knows the whole story.

I tried to find out who wrote Genesis, but nobody seems to know for sure. Obviously it has been a long time, so it's very difficult to figure out who did the interviews and who wrote things down and who edited it all. Whoever it was wrote very fast and left things out. Some of the paragraphs they wrote sound like a postcard from your kid at camp.

There are biblical scholars who believe the book of Genesis was written by several different writers, with Moses acting as an editor for not only Genesis but also other books of the Bible, including Deuteronomy. But it would've been difficult for Moses to write Deuteronomy because of chapter 34, verse 5:

And Moses the servant of the Lord died there in Moab, as the Lord had said.

I don't think Moses wrote that.

And in the next verse it says:

God buried him in Moab, in the valley opposite Beth Peor, but to this day no one knows where his grave is.

Exactly! The writers left out where Moses was buried. Or maybe the editor cut it out. Somewhere in Moab? That covers a lot of area. Of course, God knows where Moses is buried (here we go again, God only knows), and he must've told the writers, but they didn't put it in the Bible. Was anyone doing fact checking? Where was the publisher at the time?

So the one thing we know about Genesis is that we don't know for certain who wrote it. But we do know the writer and the editor and the publisher and the accountant are all hooked up in this somewhere.

Genesis starts out great. The writers tell us that God created the Heavens and the Earth. And he created the animals and the plants and everything that exists today. And I'm happy about all that because it makes sense to me and I believe. It's very precise and the writers didn't leave anything out. The writers even tell us how long it took— six days—and that God rested on the seventh day.

Rested? God *rested*? Hello? Writers? God rested? What are you saying here, writers? God never rested because he never got tired. You're talking about God resting when every pastor speaking of God preaches that God never rests.

So after God made the Heavens and the Earth, the writers tell us that God said:

Let us make man in our image, after our likeness.

I'm not going to question anything, but I'm just going to ask a question. Who was God talking to? Are the writers giving God invisible friends? The writers left that out. Then, a few lines later, the writers say that God said:

So God created man in his own image.

So which was it? "Our image" or "his own image"? A good editor would've caught that. (If you wrote a letter to the editor in those times, you probably would've gotten the same response you'd get today: *We stand behind our reporting.*)

So God created man, and the first thing God said to Adam was:

Don't eat the fruit from the tree in the middle of the garden.

(I'm not sure, but I think this is the first and only time God used the word "don't.")

Leaving the fruit alone was no problem for Adam. From the moment he met God, Adam just did whatever God said. Adam was good. Adam was wonderful. A wonderful human being. He didn't argue; he just did it. There are no long conversations between God and Adam. No debates. God says do; Adam does. So when God said don't eat the fruit, Adam had no intention of eating the fruit. Besides, there must've been other fruit in the garden. So what did Adam eat? Not a word about that.

Missing pages!

When I do a television show, the writers bring pages to the set every day. And the producers check to make sure there are no pages missing. The writers and editors of Genesis didn't seem to do any of that. If I went to any of the seven networks and handed them Genesis and said, "This guy has written a spec outline for a new show," they'd want to know where the characters are going to be in episode 89 and then pass on the whole project.

So there's Adam sitting in the garden when God started bringing animals to him:

Out of the ground the Lord God formed every beast of the field and every bird of the air, and brought them to the man to see what he would call them; and whatever the man called every living creature, that was its name.

I'm not sure how many animals there were back then—today there are more than fifty thousand different species—but Adam named them all. And God made them all.

Aha! Ohhhh! So *that's* why God rested. Fifty thousand species! Male and female. That's one hundred thousand animals. And God did all of that in six days. *Now* I understand why God rested. Anybody would've. Never mind, I think you get it. I feel like resting right now just thinking about it.

Adam must've gotten tired naming fifty thousand species. He was human, and being a human being, he had to nod off every now and then, but God kept coming and coming and waking him up. And if you look at some of the animal names, I believe there's proof that God woke Adam up and Adam was startled. I can imagine God waking Adam up and showing him an animal and saying, *Name this!* And one time when God woke Adam up, Adam just blurted out, *Sloth!*

And God asked, *How do you spell it?*

Then God held up another animal. *Name this one!*

Adam asked, *What does it do?*

God said, *It eats ants.*

Anteater! Adam said; then he went back and took another nap.

I defy you to come up with a word like "sloth." Or "manatee." "Wombat." "Barramundi." "Armadillo." You name it, Adam named it. But he had plenty of time. There wasn't much else to do in the garden.

The picture of God enjoying himself, going off somewhere that cannot be seen, God walking and enjoying putting together the anatomy, the physiology, and everything that goes into making an animate object. Fifty thousand species, male and female, and bringing them to Adam. And Adam, this servant of God, and God must have had a conversation, gained a familiarity over this period of time. I can see God holding up two animals and hear Adam saying:

Beavers!

And God says, *Okay! Beavers!*

And Adam can't wait to see what God will bring next. I can see God smiling and bringing two more animals to be named and wondering, *Now, what is he going to call this?* And Adam asking, *Is that the front or the back?* Imagine God, smiling and energized and happy— probably the most fun God has had in a long time— knowing that he likes Adam, his creation, a man in his own image. Just imagine! God and Adam having a wonderful time. Not as two men but as God and man. No sin, no corruption, no violence, no drinking, no smoking. Just making animals and laughing. Maybe the only time God laughed.

Because of the missing pages, we have to imagine for ourselves whether God put the animals down and they ran away or God took them away after Adam named them. The writers just don't tell us, and they don't tell us the names of the animals in Genesis. So how do we know what Adam called the animals? Maybe he wrote them down and somebody found the names later. But the

writers don't say if Adam had anything to write with. I'm thinking that one of the animals was a cockatoo. Whatever Adam said, the cockatoo repeated. When the cockatoo flew from the garden, that's when we got the names, because the press was waiting outside the gate.

Now this guy Adam, who is actually the first person

to see things, has seen everything, but he has never seen a woman. He has no idea anything like that exists. He wasn't even sure about the word "mate." I mean, what is he supposed to do with a helpmate? I think Adam may have been a little bit concerned. We're not sure if he'd seen any animals mating, because the writers didn't put any of that in there.

Missing pages!

And Adam must've thought, *Here we were, having a good time making animals and naming them, and now God says I need a helpmate?* Adam knew nothing except he was having fun and all of a sudden: *You need a helpmate.*

What did Adam say to God about having a help-mate? Did Adam just say: *Okay?* Or did he say, *Okay, but I don't want a boss?* We'll never know because the writers didn't write that down.

Missing pages!

So God said to Adam, *You need a helpmate.* Now God goes off. (I don't know if it's like show business and God walks off into a fog of blue smoke and then comes out with something.) All Adam knew is that God said, *You need a helpmate.* And Adam had watched when God actually made things and brought them back for Adam to name, and they were all so different. A mouse. A giraffe. A frog. A walrus. All different. So Adam had no idea what God was going to bring back. God could've brought back a chamois.

Here, Adam.

What is it?

It's a chamois. And it'll hold a cubit of water. You can wring it out and it's dry and you can sop and mop.

There's no conversation between God and Adam describing this helpmate, and therefore Adam has no idea what "helpmate" means. Or maybe Adam did have an idea because these other animals that he named — there's a male and a female, male sloth, female sloth — were in pairs, so now he would have someone too. A helpmate. For him. We'll never know which it was, because the writers left that out too.

Missing pages!

After telling Adam he needed a helpmate, the next thing that happens is:

The Lord God caused a deep sleep to fall upon the man, and while he slept took one of his ribs.

God plucked a rib from Adam. And God was very good at that. But why did God need a rib to make a woman? I have no idea, because nowhere do the writers mention God using anything but dirt to make Adam and all the animals.

Once again, because there are so many missing pages, I can only assume that God spoke with Eve before he took her to meet Adam. I also think God told Eve wonderful things about Adam and she was looking forward to meeting him. Maybe she fixed herself up—

I'm not talking about lipstick, just the hair—and she asked God, *How do I look?* And God said, *You look fine. Let's go meet him.*

When Eve arrives, Adam is asleep. I can only assume that God is standing there with her. We don't know for sure.

Once again, more missing pages!

So God calls unto Adam, I assume, and wakes him up and says, *Behold!* And there's Eve standing there. But Eve is not happy. Why? Because she got all fixed up and when she finally meets Adam, the guy is napping, which bothered her greatly. Remember, Eve is human—a woman— and this is the first time we see a woman not happy. I won't say she was angry; I will say she was not happy. And to this day, women still have Eve DNA in them.

Those of us who are married more than three decades know wives don't really appreciate it if you nap. In fact, wives hate to see their husbands napping. When a wife finds her husband on the sofa napping, the wife clenches her fists, looks to the Heavens, and bites down on her teeth. These are the actions and motions of a person who wants to kill something just because she sees a man napping. People feel warm and fuzzy when they see a baby napping, but wives want to kill when they see their husbands napping on the sofa. Which is great for the home-furnishing business. Stores sell thousands of pillows to wives so they can cover the sofa to keep the husband from getting on it. And these pillows don't match the color of anything.

All because wives have Eve DNA in them.

So Adam woke up—we don't know if God woke him up or he woke up by himself, because the writers left that out—and he saw this woman who wasn't there before. Keep in mind that Adam named all the animals, so the minute he saw this woman he knew there was a difference. And I would imagine—when he woke up, not used to speaking with anybody except God, and he saw God standing there with a woman, he thought he was dreaming. And I would further imagine that Adam was so quick at naming things from habit—after you go through fifty thousand of God's species, you really do develop a knack for it—but this time it wasn't a name; it was an expression.

Whoa! Man!

And that's how woman got the name. It's pronounced differently today, but that's how it happened back then. Adam saw that she was beautiful and that this was his mate. *Whoa! Man!*

I don't know what God promised Eve about this fellow, but I think it's safe to say that Adam didn't really know how to talk to a woman. All Adam knew was that God had taken a rib from him to make her. So when he did his welcome-to-the-garden speech, he called her "bone of my bones." And I think this is the first time any human ever said, *Oh God!* That's what Eve said, *Oh God!* And Adam, upon seeing that Eve wasn't really all that impressed with "bone of my bones," went deeper and called her "flesh of my flesh" And Eve said, *Oh God!* Which was the second time a human said, *Oh God!*

But how did the first female go from being named woman to being named Eve? Our friends the writers and editors and publishers and, of course, our friend the bottom-line man, the accountant, claiming not enough space, left that part out, so we'll never know where she got the name Eve. All Genesis says is this:

The man called his wife's name Eve, because she was the mother of all living creatures.

Maybe Eve meant "mother of all living" back then. I don't know.

So now Eve has moved in. But we don't see her saying anything about the way things look. When a woman moves in, it becomes *her* house. But the writers don't get into that conversation between Adam and Eve.

Eve: What are those sticks doing all over the ground?
Adam: They fell off the trees.
Eve: Pick them up.
Adam: Why?
Eve: Because I can't live in this mess.

A male can step over things. A female can't. So Eve walks around complaining and making corrections and changing everything in the place where Adam used to live. Fixing things the way she wants them. Where was Adam? No mention of where he went. I would imagine he was off someplace just sitting and thinking that he's not bothering anybody.

The next thing the writers tell us is that Eve talked to the serpent. Now, God must've told her not to eat the fruit from the tree in the middle of the garden. I'm sure God was clear about that and said something like: *If you eat that fruit you're going to become wise, but you will surely die.* But the serpent talked her into eating the fruit.

Hark! Stop right there. Why did the serpent talk to Eve and not Adam? Didn't any of the animals talk to Adam? He named all these animals; how come none of

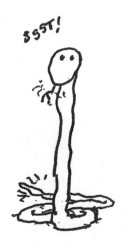

them talked to him? There is nothing written about Adam talking to any of the animals great and small, with or without a shell.

Nothing talked to Adam? What did Adam do before Eve got there? Just sit in the garden without talking to anything? Not one thing—there's no report—I'm not saying it didn't happen, but why did the writers leave that out? Adam should have had a conversation with something. Birds. Something. I mean, Tarzan started to communicate with the animals right away and used the same sound to call a thousand elephants that he used to call thousands of lions. Tarzan could summon a lot of things. But then that's Edgar Rice Burroughs, a writer who didn't leave things out. Plus, I think he had a better editor. Then again, he's not quoted on Sunday mornings.

Females see things differently than males. When God told Adam not to eat the fruit, he was okay with that. But Eve, being a woman, probably thought, *Why can't you eat this fruit?* This makes sense because we know that the serpent told Eve it was all right to eat the forbidden fruit and Eve plucked one from the tree and ate it. Then she took a piece of fruit back to Adam and said, *Eat this.*

It's here where I feel really sorry for Adam. If God tells you to do something and your wife tells you to do something else, what should you do? Adam has never had an argument—not with God, not with his wife—so he has to figure out which would be worse. Adam chose not to start something with his wife and ate the fruit. I think Adam may have rationalized this because he wasn't there—he didn't hear the conversation Eve had with the serpent—so when Eve said *Eat this,* he ate it because he remembered God saying, *You need a help-mate.* And so Adam thought, *Okay, this is my helpmate—the helpmate God gave to me—and so I'll eat the fruit.*

As the writers of Genesis tell us:

And she also gave some to her husband, and he ate. Then the eyes of both were opened, and they knew that they were naked; and they sewed fig leaves together.

But it seems Adam knew this was the fruit from the tree in the middle of the garden because he later must explain to God why he ate it. Adam knew this was the forbidden fruit and he watched Eve eat it. There he is looking at his helpmate eating forbidden fruit, and there's no mention of him trying to stop her. He could've said, *Hark! God said don't eat of the fruit of the tree in the middle of the garden!* Yes, he could've said, *Hark!* Which was a big word then in stopping things.

But he didn't.

Or he could've squealed like a three year old:

Ooooooo! I'm telling!

And then Adam could have gone to God and said, *Go ahead. Help yourself. I've got another rib.*

But Adam didn't do that either. He ate of the forbidden fruit.

After eating the fruit, Adam knew good and evil. What does that mean? This working man who does what God says and there's no trouble. But now he knows the difference between good and evil and he's ashamed. Eve is ashamed too. So they sewed leaves together because they were naked and wanted to cover themselves.

But why cover yourself if everything else is naked? There's nothing else walking around covered. Nothing else is embarrassed. When God created these things, the word "naked" was not there. And I suppose the animals are not wearing leaves because they hadn't eaten any of the fruit. We can only imagine that if the animals had eaten of the fruit, what fifty thousand species would look like trying to use a needle and thread and covering themselves and putting flaps on the back. Of course, some of them didn't need a flap on the back because they had a tail.

Let me remind you again: There have to be some missing pages, because the writers don't say anything about where Eve got the needle and thread to sew the leaves together. Or even the words "needle and thread." I can picture a man saying "hook and ladder," but I can't think of a man saying "needle and thread."

So Eve must've said, *Get me some needle and thread.* But Adam couldn't find either of those things.

Adam (calling from a distance): Where did you say it was?

Eve: Oh, never mind, I'll get it myself.

Even today, if you asked a husband to find needle and thread, he could not. So it had to be Eve who came up with the needle and thread. Obviously a wife could find needle and thread, not a husband. Especially if she's ashamed.

Let's assume it was Eve who found the needle and thread, and then she sent Adam out for some leaves. Now, when you think of leaves—one's mind when reading can only go to that which one has seen—you can only imagine the leaves that fall from the tree at your house or when you walk through the park. I'm sure everybody's picturing tree leaves, but who knows what was growing in those days. According to the film *One Million B.C.*, there were some huge leaves back then. I called the botanical garden and asked the guy there how big leaves grow these days, and he said there is a tree called raphia farinifera, which has leaves more than sixty-five feet across. Adam could have dragged a leaf like that back.

Eve: What is that?
Adam: It's a leaf.
Eve: Where'd you get that?
Adam: Over by the pond.

Eve: It's too big.
Adam: Can't you cut it?
Eve: We don't have scissors. Go back and find something
smaller.

A few minutes later, Adam comes back with half a
beehive.

Adam: Is this better?
Eve: No, that's not a leaf. That's a beehive. What am I
supposed to do with a beehive?
Adam: Use it to cover yourself.
Eve: What about the bees?
Adam: Oh.
Eve: Leaves, Adam. Leaves. Now, go and find some
small leaves.

Eventually, the writers tell us, they settled on fig
leaves. Eve sewed them together and they were now covered thereof. (The word "thereof" covers a whole lot.) It
seems to me that this thing about the leaves established
the positioning between the two of them and also
between all husbands and wives. Women are always
sending their husbands out to find something or bring
something back home. During that certain time of the
year called fall, when the wife finds the husband napping on the couch, she tells him to go outside and rake

the leaves that have fallen from the tree and are now all over the yard.

Eve DNA! Napping and leaves. Two definite links between the wife today and Eve.

You'll also notice, when wives ask you to do something, they don't say "will you," they say "can you." *Can you come here for a minute and do this*? And the husband says, *Okay. I will*. This is the mantra of the husband — *I will*. The mantra of the wife in response to *I will* is not *When* but *Now!*

So God walks through the garden. The writers wrote that God was walking. I don't know if there's a description like that anywhere else in the Bible, anything about God walking or God came walking. I've always thought of God as a spirit, a voice. Were Adam and Eve able to see God? The writers left that part out. Moses, Noah, all of them heard God, but did they see God? Were Adam and Eve the only people to see God?

Missing pages!

The writers say Adam and Eve heard God walking in the garden. Normally Adam would've smiled and said, *Here comes God!* But now Adam and Eve are ashamed. They have the leaves on and they took a position behind some bushes or whatever, hiding from God, who is walking in his garden. I must repeat: They are *hiding* from God in *God's* garden. Obviously the fruit hadn't kicked in yet.

And then they hear the voice of God:

God: Where are you?

God already knows where they are. This is the parallel of parenting because like any parent, God already knows the answer to every question. God never asks a question without knowing the answer. Like my mother. We didn't have a telephone, so nobody could've told her what I had done. She would ask a question: *Where were you?* But she already knew the answer. She already knew I had gone someplace I was not supposed to go. And how did she know all this? She blamed it on a little bird. And I've always been confused about that little bird. But then, after talking to other people who used to be, at one time in their lives, children, it seems this little bird had relatives or it was a big business where mothers all chipped in to pay little birds. And these birds are everywhere in any language you want.

So Adam answers God's question— *Where are you?*

Adam: I heard the sound of thee in the garden, and I was afraid, because I was naked; and I hid myself.

If he was naked, what happened to the leaves? When he said this, I can only assume his leaves had fallen off, maybe while he was running to hide. After all, this was the first time Eve ever sewed anything, so maybe she didn't do a good job with the needle and thread.

Adam, whom I can picture crouching behind a bush, stood and said he was afraid because he was naked. To which God replied:

God: Who told you that you were naked?

I can see right there that the writers of Genesis had no comedy instinct, because the direct answer should have been:

Adam: My leaf fell off.

But God probably would've ignored Adam's punch line anyway because Genesis is not Neil Simon.

According to the writers, God then said:

Behold, the man has become like one of us, knowing good and evil.

Us? Here again, who are these other people God is talking to? The writers never tell us.

Missing pages!

Adam, seeing that God is putting everything on him, immediately comes clean and makes an honest statement:

Adam: The woman whom thou gavest to be with me, she gavest me fruit of the tree, and I ate.

In other words, Adam is telling God he thought it was all right to eat the fruit. Okay, here she comes, he names her woman, she becomes Eve because of so forth and so on, and then she goes off and eats the fruit. What is a man supposed to do when this is the woman God has given to him? When Adam eats the fruit, there is no snake to tell him, *Thoust will be this or thoust will be that.* Plus there weren't yet warning signs like heavy rain and a flood, so Adam figured everything was wonderful and it must be okay to eat the fruit. There are a lot of pages missing here, but that's my guess about what Adam was thinking.

In defense of Adam eating the fruit, I was very proud of Adam when he stood up and said, *The woman whom thou gavest to be with me, she gavest me fruit of the tree, and I ate.* That line clarified for me the relationship between Adam and God. Adam was able to say to God he was ashamed and explain why he ate the fruit. As far as I'm concerned, this is one of the great moments in the Bible. But the writers didn't report the whole conversation, which I would imagine went on from there:

God: What are you wearing?
Adam: Leaves.
God: Didn't I tell you not to —
Adam: Now, wait a minute…

Of course, there was no word called "minute" or any word that signified time or anything, but if there were I think Adam would have said, *Wait a minute!*

Adam: Now, wait a minute! This is the woman you sent me. You brought her to me, and when I woke up she was there with you. This is the woman you said was my mate, and you were with her and you made her. I figured since you made her and then I saw her eat and I didn't see any change in her and she said have some of this and I ate it because I thought it was okay. Now it's too late and we've eaten of the fruit. Look, I know what you said, but then you went and made this woman. You brought her here and I thought you already had a talk with her about the fruit. Did you have a conversation with her about the fruit?

God: Yes.

Adam: Okay. But she didn't listen, because when she came back from a walk in the garden, behold, she was eating the fruit.

God: What did she say?

Adam: She said: Eat this. And being a good husband and knowing that if I didn't eat it there would be trouble from her, I ate it.

God: So you just ate it?
Adam: At first I said no, but then she said: Don't you
*   trust me? So I thought it must be okay to eat it.*

God turned toward Eve.

God: What is this that you have done?
Eve: The serpent beguiled me, and I ate.

Ladies and gentlemen, I want you to understand, this
is woman. And I can see her getting off her knees and
crawling out from behind the bush and standing up,
whether her leaf is falling off or not, I don't know, and she
looks at these two males—don't forget there's God and
Adam, who is in God's image, so there are two males—
and she will not have any more of this. And here we have
the first woman going up against two males. The *only* two
males. (We don't know what the snake was.) And if I
know women, when God tried talking over Eve, she said:

Eve: No, you listen to me!

And that's when God piled all that stuff on her:

God: Because you do not play well with others, you shall
*   bear the fruit and you shall have great pains when*
*   you bear the fruit.*

And Adam got hit with:

God: You shall toil in the fields and come home and say
where's my dinner?

You don't mess with God. If you do, God will put something on you.

Man: I don't feel like doing that.
God: Locusts!
Man: But I don't want to do it.
God: Famine!

Next, God cursed the serpent:

The Lord God said to the serpent, because you have done
this, cursed are you above all cattle, and above all
wild animals; upon your belly you shall go, and dust
you shall eat all the days of your life.

Which brings up another thing the writers left out: What did the serpent look like before God turned it into a crawling-on-the-belly thing? The serpent had to have looked different before God cursed it. Maybe it was a tripod with a head. I don't know. And what kind of serpent was it? Was it a python? Was it a rattler? Was it a cobra?

Missing pages!

The pictures I've always seen have the serpent hanging from a tree with Eve holding the fruit. To me, a person who has for years dealt with filming and telling the story in movies, it's a better shot for the camera operator to put the serpent in a tree as opposed to Eve standing and talking to this thing on the ground. If it's crawling on its belly, it could not rise for the close-up. Unless it was a cobra, which could come up about a foot and a half, then span itself out. That's why John Huston and Orson Welles and Alfred Hitchcock put it in a tree. It's a better close-up. But it's a better curse to have it crawling on the ground.

Looking at the anatomy of a snake, it's like when a puppeteer puts his hand in the back of a puppet, the mouth just goes up and down, so if you have no sound it seems like the thing is saying *mop, mop, mop, mop, mop.* How did the snake talk? With its forked tongue? If the snake's mouth goes up and down and that's all, how did Eve understand it? Even the eyes of the snake—there's no expression in the eyes of a snake.

I have a feeling that this was not the first time the snake had done something wrong. Because it just seems to me that after the snake had the conversation with Eve and then God came and cursed the snake, it doesn't sound like the first time the snake had been in trouble with God. For the snake to be already slithering around and for God to double it up and say now it has to crawl on it's belly, it seems to me, to *me*, that the snake had done something very bad before. Maybe this was the fourth time God cursed the snake. At least it is my belief, *my* belief, that this is at least the fourth time the serpent has been cursed. But I do think it learned its lesson and never did anything bad again, because God's next curse probably would have been: *You will crawl on your back.*

And let me say that I believe this is not the only animal that God may have cursed. But these other curses have been left out of Genesis.

Missing pages!

What other animals did God curse? If you go to a zoo, for instance, and see a baboon, the first thing baboons do is turn themselves around and show you a certain inflamed area of their body. One can imagine that God could have said to the baboon:

From now on you shalt haveth an exposed and inflamed part of your body that you will show to people.

The *penguin*? Whatever the penguin was before it got in trouble with God, I don't know. I can imagine God saying to the penguin:

And thou shalt go through life with no knees and your behind very low to the ground.

At least God was very merciful, putting a penguin's behind low to the ground so that when it fell it didn't fall too far. On the other hand, it doesn't have a real bark and it can't attack. Nor can it run away fast. On land. It has wings and it can't fly. It really is disturbing. Poor penguin. Though I don't know if we can call it poor or not because we don't know what the penguin did that annoyed God so much. But whatever it was, God did these things to the penguin. And God cursed the penguin even more:

And thou shalt have duck feet and look like you're wearing a tux but be rejected by gourmet restaurants and expensive hotels because you have no bow tie. And thou shalt have your image used in advertising for a menthol cigarette which gives human beings cancer.

After God cursed Adam and Eve and the snake, the next thing that happened, according to the writers, was this:

And now, lest he put forth his hand and take also of the tree of life, and eat, and live forever, therefore the Lord God sent him forth from the Garden of Eden, to till the ground from which he was taken. He drove out the man; and at the east of the Garden of Eden he placed the cherubim, and a flaming sword which turned every way, to guard the way to the tree of life.

Cherubim? Who named that thing? Cherubim.

There's no description of cherubim in Genesis, so I had to call a minister I know and ask him, what are cherubim? The minister told me cherubim have four faces: a lion, an ox, a vulture, and a man. They have the hands of a man, the feet of a calf, and four wings. Not a creature you'd want to fool around with. If you went to visit a neighbor's house and they had some of those things in the yard, there is no way you're going to open that gate. Even if the cherubim are quiet and not making a noise, you don't want to bother these things. They've got wings, so you don't even make the approach. If you're the mailman or UPS or FedEx—whoever's delivering sort of tosses the package over the fence and keeps going. As a matter of fact, you don't even get out of the truck. And nothing that says "Dear Occupant" ever gets delivered.

If you've been thrown out of a place that has a flaming sword and cherubim at the front gate, there's no way you're going to want to come back home. (I have no idea what the flaming sword can do to you, but it will keep you busy watching it.)

At least God gave Adam and Eve something to wear besides leaves before he put them out:

And the Lord God made for Adam and for his wife garments of skins, and clothed them.

Skins from *what*? But then again, God could make skins and it didn't have to come off of anything.

It seems to me, Adam and Eve marked the beginning of parenting. After that there were Moses, Noah, and a plethora of people whom God chose to go forth and do things, and they were not afraid to say to God: *This is not working.* To be chosen by God is not necessarily a great deal of fun. Chosen by God, judged by humans. Not fun. When God lights a bush and the flames spew out, that's not fun to explain to somebody. It's not fun. God says, *Go do so forth or so on.* And since you're chosen, you have to do it. You're not supposed to ask God, *Why am I doing this?* You just do it. Like Moses, telling people, *Go ahead. The water's going to part.* Or Noah building an ark. Or David, who must have heard how big Goliath was and that he was coming. Didn't matter. God told David to go up against Goliath. And this is way before the song "Don't Worry, Be Happy."

The fact that God, the first parent, threw Adam and Eve out of the garden is proof he didn't have a wife. And the fact that they never came back into the garden is further proof that God didn't have a wife because the mother of the children would have made God bring them back. And the conversation would've gone something like this:

God's wife: What did you do with the children?
God: I put 'em out.
God's wife: You did what?

God: I told you, I threw them out.
God's wife: For what?
God: They ate of the tree.
God's wife: I told you, ask me first. Now, go get those
children and bring them back in.

I don't know much about cockatoos, but I'm guessing that by the time God was casting Adam and Eve out of the garden, the cockatoo was probably losing it trying to remember fifty thousand species. I can picture the cockatoo's head bobbing up and down and the cockatoo repeating the same animal names over and over and even some names that didn't exist. And God, seeing this, would've said to Adam, *Don't forget, you've got to write down the names of all these animals. Get your helpmate to help you with that.*

And being a married man all of my life, I can only imagine that on the way through the gate, Eve turned to Adam and said, *I don't care what happens, I'm going to get you. If it's the last thing I do, I'm going to get you.*

Obviously, to be continued . . .

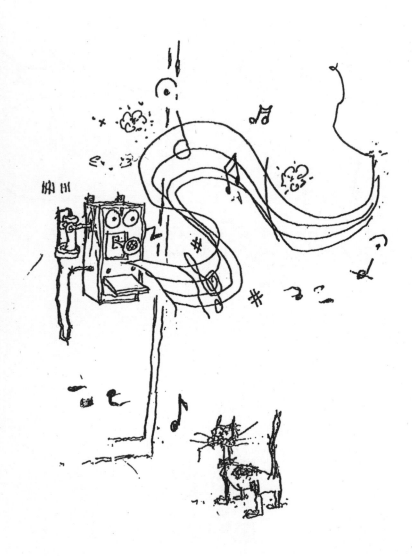

VOICE MAIL

I have a friend. A singer. When I decided to call him the
other day, I got his voice mail. First I heard the recording of a woman:

Good morning, you've reached the office of…

And suddenly my friend started singing:

Stevie's private number!

And then the woman came back and said:

Please say your full name.

"Bill Cosby."

After that, her voice came back:

He left a note saying…

Then my friend was back singing his phone number
and singing a message, which was:

*I'm not available to take your call at this time. But if
you leave your name, and number of telephone, I promise
to call you back…you back…you back…you back…you
baaaack…*

Then the woman's voice again:

He told me to cover the phone for him. Is it urgent? Yes or no?

"No."

Would you like to leave a message? Yes or no?

"Yes."

Okay. First I need your area code and phone number. Please enter it using touchtone, followed by the pound key.

I wasn't fast enough.

First I need your area code and phone number. Say the digits one by one. Or use touchtone and end with the pound key.

I said my number slowly.

Now you can leave your message and hang up or press pound. Go ahead.

"Yes. This is George Washington Carver and I'm wondering if I can get a phone number for Bill Cosby."

Got it! Hang up or press pound to send it. Otherwise, to hear your message, press one. To rerecord it, press two.

I pressed the wrong button, and she said:

Okay, I'll mark it urgent. Hang up or press pound to send it. Otherwise, to hear your message, press one.

I pressed pound.

I'll get this to him as soon as possible. Thanks for calling. Good-bye.

You see, that's the problem with technology. You can have a conversation with a person who isn't a person. And be interviewed by a friend of yours who isn't there.

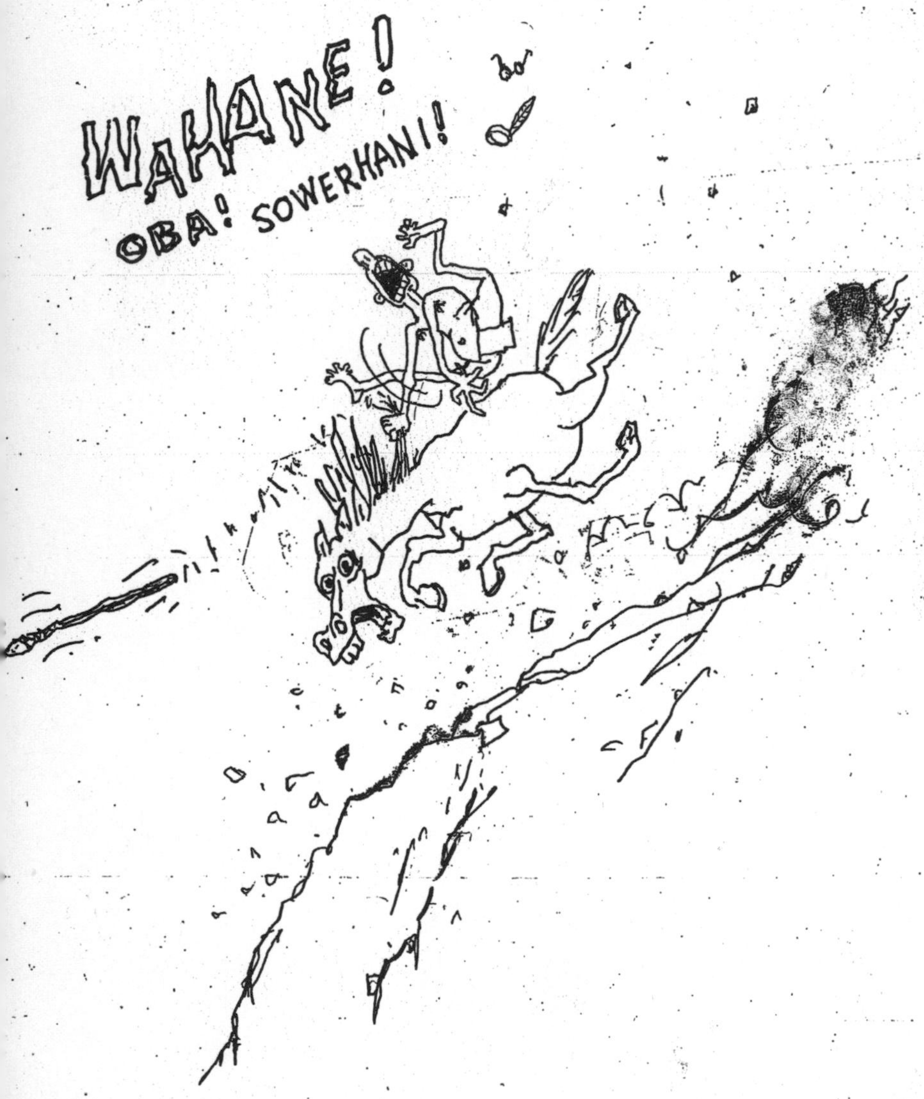
WAHANE!
OBA! SOWERHANI!

IF ONLY NATIVE AMERICANS KNEW *THEN* WHAT THEY KNOW *NOW*

Most of what I know about how the West was won is because of actors like Randolph Scott, John Wayne, Joel McCrea, Gary Cooper, Ward Bond, George "Gabby" Hayes, and Fuzzy Knight. And directors John Ford and Howard Hawks. Stories about real-life characters Wild Bill Hickok and Annie Oakley. It seems that back in the days of the Wild West, there was a lot of fighting— Native Americans riding down from the hills and attacking covered wagons.

At least that's what you see in the movies. And when I watched those movies, I often wondered why the Native Americans couldn't be quieter as opposed to the loud yelping sounds that they were making. After a thorough investigation within my own mind, I think that with no saddle, just a blanket, and no jockstrap, that if one is bouncing up and down on the spine, the hard, broad bone of a horse, up and down, maybe three or four inches at a time, there is a tendency for one to land on the two very important parts of the male anatomy, which — I don't care how strong you are, how brave — would bring a yelp. So you have hundreds of males, Native American males, yelping as they ride toward the wagons. They were called "braves," but I don't think the yelping had anything to do with a great spirit. These guys are getting killed bouncing on themselves. And so they come yelping, and by the time they get to the wagons, they are very, very upset, and so they start to shoot. Then they have to go around the wagons a couple times and there is more bouncing and yelping.

If only Native Americans knew *then* what they know *now*...

So this is what I saw sitting in the Booker Movie, which was a neighborhood movie house, and the Astor and Jumbo on Girard Avenue. Sitting there in the theater for ten cents. To this day I will not have any of the black Jujyfruit because I don't know what flavor the black Jujyfruit is supposed to be. All I know is when somebody bought a box of Jujyfruit, you could find the black ones all over the floor. And people threw them at the screen too. When they didn't like the character, the black Jujyfruit started flying. If someone could please text or tweet what flavor I'm supposed to be tasting, I'd appreciate it. And please don't tell me I'm supposed to be tasting black. I don't know what flavor that is.

Another thing I've wondered about when watching

Westerns is whether or not the settlers had to practice pulling their wagons into a circle. You never see them practice anything in the movies, but when the Native Americans come riding down the hill, the settlers all seem to know what to do. It is my belief—although I've never seen it in the movies—they had to have practiced. I can imagine the leader, whose name is Pathfinder, standing in front of all these settlers and their covered wagons.

> *Pathfinder: All right, ladies and gentlemen, here we go, pots and pans and everything, pull them in. And we are going to be in a straight line and when you hear me yell, "Pork chop," then Sarge will ride quickly down yelling "Indians, Indians, Indians."*

(Sarge is not really in the army or anything anymore; his name is just Sarge.)

> *Pathfinder: The drivers will quickly move around to form a circle. I will count, and what we're looking for is no longer than eight seconds to make the full circle. The women, those who want to, will grab a rifle and go under the wagons alongside the men. Children will stay in the wagons behind the bags of flour, which, hopefully, will block the bullets. Stay down, remember that. Take all the water, which is very valuable, and put it inside if you can. And*

if you can't cover yourself behind the bags of flour, then use the water because whatever they shoot may not penetrate the water jugs. Remember, folks, this all must be done by the count of eight. All right? Now, don't forget, no cheating. We're staying calm, just looking around, looking at trees and things.

And I can imagine Pathfinder riding back and forth to make sure everybody's doing what they're supposed to do. Also, at the end of the line, there's somebody named Leonard, who is the pickup man. What he does is, he walks along to pick up things that have fallen off of wagons.

At some point, Pathfinder yells:

Pathfinder: Pork chop!

And then Sarge rides up very fast.

Sarge: Indians, Indians, Indians, Indians!
Pathfinder: Okay, now! Here we go! Just stay calm!
One, two, three, four!

And they start. The drivers all make a right turn. But this is the first time they ever did it, and since nobody gave them exact instructions, the first wagon made a right turn and the last wagon made a left turn, and they wound up with the last wagon being out there by itself.

> *Pathfinder: We've got to stop this! Now, everybody, here we go, everybody listen carefully. When we say Indians, everybody follow the first wagon until we make a complete circle. Okay, now, here we go, everybody in a single line.*

And I can hear the music from *Gunsmoke* or something playing. The first driver is a little fast—he pulls out yelling "yah, yah, yah"—and the wagons are all going but the only problem is everybody is moving fast and the last wagon can't catch up with the first wagon.

> *Pathfinder: Okay! Everybody stop—we got to figure this out! Lead wagon will take off first and the others will follow, and you will not stop until you get to the last wagon, and that will make the circle. This is very, very difficult to do because if the first wagon moves fast while the other wagons are moving along slowly, the trailing wagons probably will not catch up to the lead wagon, and instead of a circle, we'll have a U or a C. Okay, here we go again. We'll do it three times.*

So maybe the first time isn't so good, but the second time the first wagon catches up to the last wagon but there's a huge gap. Then the third time is pretty good, but even as Pathfinder continues to direct the wagons, there still is a little bit of a gap.

Pathfinder: Now, let's close this up. We have to close this up and come around. Okay, now everybody jump out with your rifles. Here we go. And point. Now form a circle, five, six, seven, eight, we have a perfect circle. Everybody under the wagons! Eleven, twelve. Now...stop!

Pathfinder gets off his horse and looks around.

Pathfinder: What is wrong with this situation? Can anybody tell me? You're all there, you've got the rifles in your hands and you're pointing. What is wrong with this picture?
Settler: Uh, we're really pointing at each other.
Pathfinder: Exactly! So let's do this. They're coming from this side, so what do you do?
Settler: Well, we'd turn around.
Pathfinder: Exactly! You turn around so you're all pointing in the same direction. At them. So whatever direction they're coming in, shoot out.
Settler: Okay.

Pathfinder: So here they come; they're coming down. Everyone under their wagon; everyone face shooting out.

Settler: I have a question. I'm under somebody's horse and the horse is not standing still — it's jumping. Is there a way to keep the horse still somehow?

Pathfinder: No. You'll just have to take your shot and aim around it.

Of course, as is always the case, a child starts crying.

Pathfinder: Can we try to keep the children quiet?

Pathfinder is getting frustrated.

Pathfinder: Can everybody get back in your wagons? And the lead wagon, we'll form a straight line again, go back, that's it, turn around, come on back, we have a straight line. Now, here we go, and that's it, stay in a straight line, everybody stay relaxed.

Once again, Sarge comes riding through.

Sarge: Indians, Indians, Indians!

And Pathfinder goes back to directing.

Pathfinder: Six, seven, eight. Great! That's a perfect circle!

The settlers jump out, and now they're all under their wagons. And they're pointing the rifles. Pathfinder rides back and forth, inspecting.

Pathfinder: That's great, great, great! Wonderful, wonderful, wonderful! And okay, perfect. Now we just have to tighten up on the timing. If we can do this in eight seconds, we'll be ready to go to Colorado.

So now they're all ready in the wagons, and according to the movies, there's always a pregnant woman and the pans are clanking and the music is playing.

Paw: Maw?
Maw: Yes, Paw?
Paw: Emmy Lou had that baby yet?
Maw: Not yet, Paw, but just keep that water boiling. Could happen anytime.

Then all of sudden we hear drums and the camera cuts to the hillside where there are all these white actors with wigs, made with hair from Pakistan and India. And they have painted faces. It was my belief, sitting in the

Booker and the Astor and Jumbo for ten cents, that the actors were told to just make something sound Native American. *Wahana! Oba! Sowerhani!* And then thrust the spear forward.

Now, in these movies, the Native Americans are always sitting way up on the hill and the wagons are coming through the valley or the pass. In fact, in every movie, the settlers always have to come through some narrow space between two mountains. And there's about a thousand Native Americans up on the top of the hill who have been waiting for the settlers. I don't know how long they've been waiting, but they're always up there when the settlers come through. We can tell it's cold because the settlers have long sleeves, long pants, and jackets. The women have bonnets. But the actors playing the Native Americans just have some beads on their chests and a piece of something to cover up the part that Adam and Eve didn't want to show. I mean, these people are just about naked except for feathers. There's no saddle on their horses, no reins. And they're using bows and arrows as weapons.

As far as I'm concerned, if you made this into an Olympic event, it would be the most difficult event ever. The rules would read something like this:

While shooting at a target with a bow and arrow, the entrant will wear no clothes and will ride downhill very fast on a horse with no saddle, reins, or stirrups.

And don't forget, movies make you think that every-thing is smooth. You hardly ever see where a horse stepped in a hole and broke its leg. That may have happened, but that's not shown. I know we must have lost many, many horses on both sides, stepping into gopher holes and gullies or whatever, but that's not in the movie.

When the Native Americans ride down the hill, how do they guide the horse? Well, they kick the horse on whatever side and the horse will make a turn that way. This is multitasking. So I feel that one can say Native Americans were the first multitaskers. Because in order to arrive at the right place when you get down the hill, you've got to point your horse in the right direction. At the same time, you're also trying to take the arrow and put the notch of the arrow onto the string. (That notch is called the "nock." I don't know why they didn't just call it the "notch.") Once you get the arrow on the string and put it in there, you have to pull on the string. Meanwhile, the horse's head is going up and down and up and down. So you have to do all this with a horse's head bobbing in your face and at the same time kick your horse to make a right turn or a left turn. And don't forget, the people are all under the wagons so you've got to bend to the left side of the horse in order to make your arrow go under the wagons.

If only Native Americans knew *then* what they know *now* . . .

History (and the movies) tells us that once the Native Americans shot somebody, they would take the scalp.

Before you start writing letters saying I'm being politically incorrect, let me explain that I'm just talking about what actually happened in those days. And thinking about that era of American history, I often wondered if Native Americans invented scalping or, if they didn't, where did they get the idea to scalp people? So I looked up scalping and found out that Native Americans did not invent scalping. Archeologists found skeletons that showed evidence of scalping in 440 BC, so it goes way back. Herodotus, the Greek historian, wrote that the Scythians of Eurasia were the first scalpers.

So the Scythians scalped. Why? Well, it was 440 BC. Obviously, nobody asked them. And there was scalping all over Europe in the ninth century, and there weren't even any rock concerts then. I mean, *everybody* was scalping. The Anglo-Saxons were big on scalping back then. So were the Visigoths. When the Spaniards came to South America, they offered money to the Mexicans for the heads of Native Americans. But then somebody said:

Look, everybody's complaining. First of all, a head is a lot to carry. And you've got to put these heads on a horse, and a lot of the horses are bucking because they don't know what you're carrying. And there are flies.

Not only was a head a lot to carry around, but it

would frighten the children. You bring the head home and the eyeballs are still loose and the tongue is hanging out and there is still stuff from the neck. And it's not like the ventriloquist where you can put your hand in there and move the mouth. *Hello, Johnny! You like this?*

So they started asking for scalps instead. Scalps were easier to carry around.

Wait a minute, we've got the Europeans—ladies and gentlemen, these are Europeans. But when I read about scalping, they separate the Spanish from the Europeans. Why? I have no idea. And the French in Canada were offering money for scalps of British soldiers. So it wasn't just the Native Americans. It was the Europeans and the almost Europeans, the Spaniards, who loaned the money to Christopher Columbus, who was a European, to come here and discover this land.

The Italians and the Portuguese are always arguing about whether Christopher Columbus was Italian or Portuguese. And some historians say that Columbus was Jewish, but I know for sure that Flip Wilson clarified history in his wonderful comedy routine telling us that if it wasn't for Christopher Columbus there would be no Ray Charles. That's something I read, although I don't know what Howard Zinn is saying about that. This is Bill Cosby speaking, not Howard Zinn. Howard Zinn told the truthful history of the United States of America and people hated him. It's like when I was saying things and people said, *Why are you bringing up our dirty laundry?*

Even the settlers were scalping Native Americans. Just go up to Boscawen, New Hampshire. You'll find a statue of a woman, Hannah Dustin, holding scalps. The way she got the scalps is this: After being captured by Native Americans, she escaped. But then she went back and killed ten Native American women and children before scalping them. And she gets a statue for doing that.

So, in the movies, everybody is running around worrying about the "savages" scalping people, when other people were scalping the so-called savages.

In the history of scalping, which was very dry reading, buried in the whole thing there's a line that says something like: There doesn't appear to be any evidence that the Eskimos scalped anybody. No explanation, just that. In thinking about the frozen north, one just could not see an Eskimo scalping anybody when you could freeze a person and feed him to the polar bear later or just leave him outside for the polar bear to find. One can't even imagine an Eskimo spending time outside scalping people. It was just too cold and the heads were probably frozen.

So whoever may have invented scalping, it is true that the Native Americans started practicing it at some point. I would imagine (or at least I would hope) that there must have been at least a couple of cavalry patrols with a major who was smart enough to realize that, given the value of scalps, if the patrol was outnumbered it would be wise to order everybody to shave their heads and ride with their hats off.

Custer cut his hair before Custer's Last Stand. This is a fact. He had those long curls. But before he rode into battle for his last stand, he cut his hair. Some people say that it wasn't unusual for him to cut his hair whenever he rode into battle, but I don't think that's true because there are drawings of him fighting with long hair. Anyway, he cut his hair before the last stand. How much, I don't know. But it worked. In a battle where the cavalry severely suffered, everybody was scalped except Custer. Which proves my theory that had they all shaved their heads, they would have been of no value and the Native Americans would have given them a pass and said, *Come back when you've grown hair.*

When I was a child, we played cowboys and Indians — that's what we called it back then. Sometimes one of us would play the Lone Ranger and one of us would be Tonto. With the help of comic books and publicity pictures — the Lone Ranger was on cereals and syrups and things like that — we knew what he looked like. (I wrote about the Lone Ranger, his trusty steed, Silver, and Tonto in the book *Cosbyology*.)

Besides comic books we had regular books. Very short books. See Tom run. The end. And then it went to another story: See the dog run. And then: The dog can run fast, which was a sequel.

We didn't have a TV. I don't mean we didn't have a TV in the house. I mean there was no TV. But I liked radio. Radio allowed me to form an image of the characters in my mind, to see them in my imagination, based on their voices. I remember how astonished I was when I first saw, in person, a fellow by the name of Uncle Wip. I had listened to his children's programs on the radio for many years. Kids could write him letters and he would give them to Santa Claus. So one day I heard that Uncle Wip was going to be in the Thanksgiving Day Parade. Since I had never actually seen Uncle Wip, I was quite excited. But when I saw him on the float, he looked nothing like the person I pictured from the voice on the radio.

So I listened to these radio shows, the all-time great shows that they now call classics. And there were all these people who were not your parents telling you stories on the radio. You see, your parents generally gave you a story after or before punishment. That's why I don't recall any great stories from my mother or father or aunt or uncle. I just don't recall those stories because I knew punishment was coming and I had no time to really pay attention.

So, yes, in a North Philadelphia housing project named after a black Episcopal bishop, Bishop Richard Allen, here we were playing cowboys and Indians. And the way we did it was quite inventive.

Of course, when you play cowboys and Indians, you have to have a horse. So each kid—I have no idea who came up with the idea, I never saw it in a drawing, I never heard about it on the radio—I just know that in the projects we took our mother's broom, stood it with the straw part up, took a rope, a rope maybe four feet long, might have even cut the rope she used to hang the wash on, brought the rope down through the middle of the straw, tied it around, and that became the reins. Then we put the stick of the broom between our legs and we rode them. Those were our horses.

Then we would take our fingers, make a fist, bring our index fingers straight out, leaving the other three fingers bent back, raise the thumb, and you've got yourself a gun. And we rode shooting at each other. I remember denying that a kid got me. He was hiding around the corner when I came riding with the stick between my legs, holding on to the reins of my mother's broom, which was now my horse. I did not name my horse like the Lone Ranger did—he was just my horse. And I had all the moves those men had Saturdays at the matinee. I could turn my horse, I could wheel it, I could have my horse still moving, still prancing, while talking to the sheriff's posse about which way we should go.

What did we look like when grown people saw us? Five or six of us riding around on brooms. All I know is that there were people who looked out the window and there were always eyes, a thousand eyes, looking around, getting ready to squeal on us: *Your son has your broom again.*

The problem was, mothers didn't like their brooms out there upside down with the top part of it being worn as it was being dragged along the cement, so some of us wound up broomless. And it wasn't as much fun without that broom for a horse. All we had were those brooms. So for some of us there was a sad day when we had no horse.

As a matter of fact, I howled with laughter when I saw Monty Python, and how those fellows pretended that they were on horseback and they didn't even have brooms. They were probably, as children, playing in the streets in lower economic areas, so I think the reason they didn't have brooms was because even in England mothers didn't like their brooms used as horses.

So there we were, five or six of us, prancing in place

while we tried to figure out who would be the cowboys and who would volunteer to be the Indians. Oddly, none of the Indians had a bow and arrow; they all had guns also. Handguns.

Obviously, the broom (the horse) couldn't be negotiated while running unless you held on to it with the rope. I also think there was some objection to the bow and arrow because nobody believed that a bow and arrow could get to you. When we saw the bow and arrow work in the movies, it was generally when the soldiers were talking to each other, and then *shoop*.

Another thing about the bow and arrow was that if you said:

Hey, Hubert, you just got an arrow through your chest.

Hubert would say:

No, they missed me.

And so you might have to argue with Hubert.

But even if they got you, there was also a magic thing in the imagination of a child playing this game of cowboys and Indians: the fix. You could get right back into play if someone just took their fingertips of both hands and went to the area where the wound was and just tapped you and said, *Fix, fix, fix.* And you were well again; you were back to life. Of course there was always some kind of argument from the Indians claiming they got one of us, and we would say, *Yeah, but we fixed him.* And then the Indians started fixing themselves. So nobody really died. It was just a lot of fun, chasing and running around.

If only Native Americans knew *then* what they know *now* ...

Yes, if only Native Americans knew then what they know now I think all the bloodshed could have been avoided. Instead of coming down the hill bouncing on horses, yelping and shooting arrows, had they gone down the hill with slot machines, set up craps tables, blackjack, or whatever, the Europeans would've started gambling and would have been broke within twenty-four hours and would've gotten on the boat and gone back where they came from.

If only Native Americans knew then what they know now ...

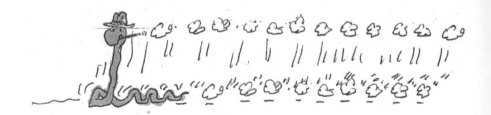

IF YOU'RE NOT
IN THE PICTURE

Mothers did not play in those days. They didn't play. There is this fellow who was the first African American basketball player in the NBA. His name is Earl Lloyd. And he tells this wonderful thing about his mother. When he was sixteen, he came home and she said:

"Where have you been?"

She already knew, so he didn't answer.

She said again, "Where have you been?"

He said, "I was just...I was just."

She said, "No, there's no 'just.' You weren't just anything. Where were you?"

He said, "I was outside."

She said, "Brilliant. Is that why you're coming in?"

By this time he knew she knew and he could feel the pressure. So he said, "Momma, please."

She said, "Now, let me ask you again. Where were you?"

He said, "I was outside."

She said, "Where?"

He said, "I was just..."

She said, "Leave this 'just' word out of everything you say. Where were you?"

He said, "I was on the corner."

She said, "Wonderful. Doing what?"

He said, "I wasn't doing anything."

She said again, "Doing what?"

He said, "I was standing there."

She said, "By yourself?"

He said, "No, ma'am."

She said, "Who were you with?"

He said, "The boy, the boy..."

She said, "You mean those boys I don't like?"

He said, "But, Momma, I wasn't doing anything!"

She said, "If you're not in the picture, you can't be framed."

ERECTILE DYSFUNCTION

What advertisers can say on television these days is way beyond me.

I remember the first time I heard the words "erectile dysfunction." It was mentioned in a television commercial. I wasn't really paying attention so I thought they were talking about some prehistoric animal. When I told my wife about it, she said:

"It's not nice to talk about the living dead."

TOO LATE FOR ME BUT
PERHAPS NOT FOR YOU

There are certain things, that our children have said to us, as parents, while trying to express themselves, that we had no answer for. At the time the child said it, we wished we had an answer. But we didn't. One of those statements was spoken after we asked our fourteen-year-old daughter to clean up her room.

"I didn't ask to be born!"

All children say it. When our daughter said it, more than thirty years ago, I didn't have an answer. At that point in time I had been dealing with hecklers my entire seventeen years of show business, yet I didn't have an answer to:

"I didn't ask to be born!"

My wife did. When my daughter said:

"I didn't ask to be born!"

My wife said:

"We didn't ask for you either."

And to this day I am still very upset because my wife

came up with it so fast. Which obviously means that her intelligence is far superior to mine. But all these years I have wanted my own answer. And I finally thought of the perfect response to:

"I didn't ask to be born!"

Now, it's too late for me to use this answer but perhaps not too late for you.

We make a mistake when we have children and think we know how to be parents. We have to understand that from birth and through a certain age there's a very fine line, even though the kid calls us Mama, Mommy, Mother, Daddy, Dada, Father, that doesn't necessarily mean anything, because these words do not have an absolute definition to the child. The child thinks that you're his or her servant because that is exactly how you respond in those first three years. You're picking up after the kid, you're cleaning the kid, you're carrying the kid. They put their arms up toward you and you pick them up. You do all of these things. You're the answer to "I want" and you're the answer to "I don't want."

"I don't want this."

"Well, you have to eat it, sweetie."

"No, I don't want it."

So this kid is the king or queen in that household, and you go along with that because the child's brain is not fully developed yet. Yes, your children are odd people. I find that it's sort of like watching people in the

Cirque du Soleil, you know, to see how double-jointed they are, but you could never do it. It's like a miracle—a person could put his foot in his mouth and it'd come out on the other side of the leg while he is standing on a piece of rope. I can't do that.

Anyway, eight hours after we told our daughter to go upstairs and clean her room, I went up and checked. She hadn't picked up a thing. So I went down and got her mother, who is my wife, and I said:

"That room is still the way it was when we told her to clean it up."

This is how it's supposed to be done. The father will tell the mother what happened, and then she will first get mad at him and then she will act accordingly with the child.

So we both went upstairs, and my daughter was in the room. Keep in mind, this was after the sixties, so there were psychological reasons not to lay a hand on your child. In fact, I agree with psychiatrist Dr. Alvin Poussaint, who was my co-author on *Come on, People*. Dr. Poussaint has always maintained that "the use of corporal punishment teaches children that violence is the way to solve problems." I think that's true. If you can find a way to explain to your child you are not your child's servant, then you, as a good parent, should do that.

But there was a time when parents, including my parents, often dispensed corporal punishment. And the first beating I got, I realized my parents were not my servants.

In the North, there was a beating, which was the only beating I knew about; that's all I knew. And to explain to those of you who don't know, the beatee has to stand still until the beater finds something with which to beat the beatee. This is rather cruel because from the beatee's viewpoint you can see a lot of things that you hope the beater does not see.

Especially an iron.

Or the ironing cord. See, it wasn't just for plugging in and heating the iron. It could put some heat on your behind. And I don't know why it was always the ironing cord, but it was.

As I said before, I am *not* in favor of corporal punishment, and I certainly wasn't in favor of it when I was on the receiving end. I'm just reporting what happened to me.

When my mother beat me, she gave an exam. And she would hit on each word or on single syllables. So she'd say:

What. Did. I. Tell. You.

Sometimes it was psychological, because I don't know what level of anger she was on, but she would say—and this was the one where I started leg movement, when she said:

You know one thing . . . ?

And never finished it.

You know one thing…?

And then:

Huh?

Getting hit on forty-seven "huhs."

Huh?…Huh?…Huh?

A good beating cannot deter you from doing the act, because you have already done it. But it sure will have you wishing you hadn't. And that's how I learned to say "I won't do it no more" real fast.

Iwon'tdoitnomore … Iwon'tdoitnomore … Iwon'tdoitnomore

Shut. Up.

There was a word that I heard—I don't know how old I was, in my thirties—and the word was "whuppin'." I'd never heard about a whuppin'. This word, "whuppin'," is from the South. And the description of a whuppin' is the strangest thing I've ever heard. A whuppin' is where the whupper gives the whuppee a knife and tells the whuppee:

Go on out yonder and cut a switch.

Now, that wasn't stupid yet, until the person said:

And bring it back.

And bring it back?

Obviously these are the laziest parents ever and the whuppee is the dumbest person I have ever heard of.

You're going to give me a knife and tell me you want

me to leave the house and go outside and cut a switch from something growing out of the ground that resembles a fishing pole or an antenna on the back of a highway patrol car and I'm going to bring it back and give it to you so you can whup me?

Noooo.

Man, I was wishing I had gotten a whuppin' instead of a beating. Once my father gave me that knife and I headed out the door, they would never see me again. My face would still be on milk cartons.

Have you seen little William? Must be around seventy-three years old now. Tell him it's all right to come home. Mom and Dad are dead.

But my mother, even though she beat me, had my best interest at heart. So did my father. I remember clearly, my drunken father, who, from time to time, in his drunkenness, did make some sense. He was the reason why I paid attention in school. Because I would come home, and in his drunkenness, the first thing he would say was:

"What class did you have today?"

I wasn't prepared to lie, so I would say, "Geometry."

"Well, what did you talk about today?"

I had to pay attention to him. Even though he didn't know what I was talking about, I had to talk about something.

"Well, Dad, today we had a wonderful day in geometry class; it was just wonderful. And this man, he had his own triangle, and his name was Hypotenuse."

My father didn't know what I was talking about.

"All right, son, go ahead on."

And he let me go. On another day, I might say, "Science."

"What'd you do today in science?' "

Since he didn't know what I was talking about, I'd respond:

"Well, today we studied leaves, Dad. Did you know there are over four hundred leaves? Listen, I will name them for you."

"Uh, never mind, thank you."

So, my wife and I are upstairs in my daughter's room. And she's sitting there, with an attitude, which the psychiatrists and psychologists have given her. And my wife said, the way mothers will:

"I thought we told you to clean up your room."

And this girl said:

"You mean the *whole* room?"

See, this is another reason why these people can't be your friends. How can they be your friends when they talk about "You mean the *whole* room?" And my wife said:

"Look!"

I was happy to hear my wife say that because I thought she only used that word with me.

Then my wife said:

"I want this cleaned up. Now!"

That's another word—"Now!" I don't know what happens, but the female, as soon as they give birth—that becomes an important word: "Now!" They want everything done "Now!"

You know, you'll be sitting around and your wife walks in the room and the conversation goes something like this:

Wife: "Look, will you go over..."
Husband: "OK, I will—"
Wife: "No! Now!"

Just as soon as they give birth, nobody's doing anything fast enough.

Now! I want it done now! You get up now! Go now! Sit down now! Stand up now! Join the church now! Now!

So when my wife told my daughter she wanted the room cleaned up *now*, my daughter said:

"I didn't ask to be born."

Well, now, this is not the first time you all have heard this, is it? They all say that. Every last one of them. And you already know how my wife responded:

"We didn't ask for you either."

As I said, I didn't have an answer at the time my daughter said "I didn't ask to be born!" (at least not one that would give me a fair chance of getting into Heaven).

But now I'm seventy-two and that daughter is forty-five years old and, at last, I have come up with the answer for myself. *My* answer. Not my wife's answer. *My* answer. And I want to give this to any of you who have teenagers who haven't yet, when you ask them to do something, said:

I didn't ask to be born.

Here's what you say:

"Yes, you did ask. Nine months before you were born, I released about sixty million, and you were one of them. So you beat out sixty million. Now, you could've hung a left, but you didn't. When you got there first, you closed the door on the others. Now, clean up your room!"

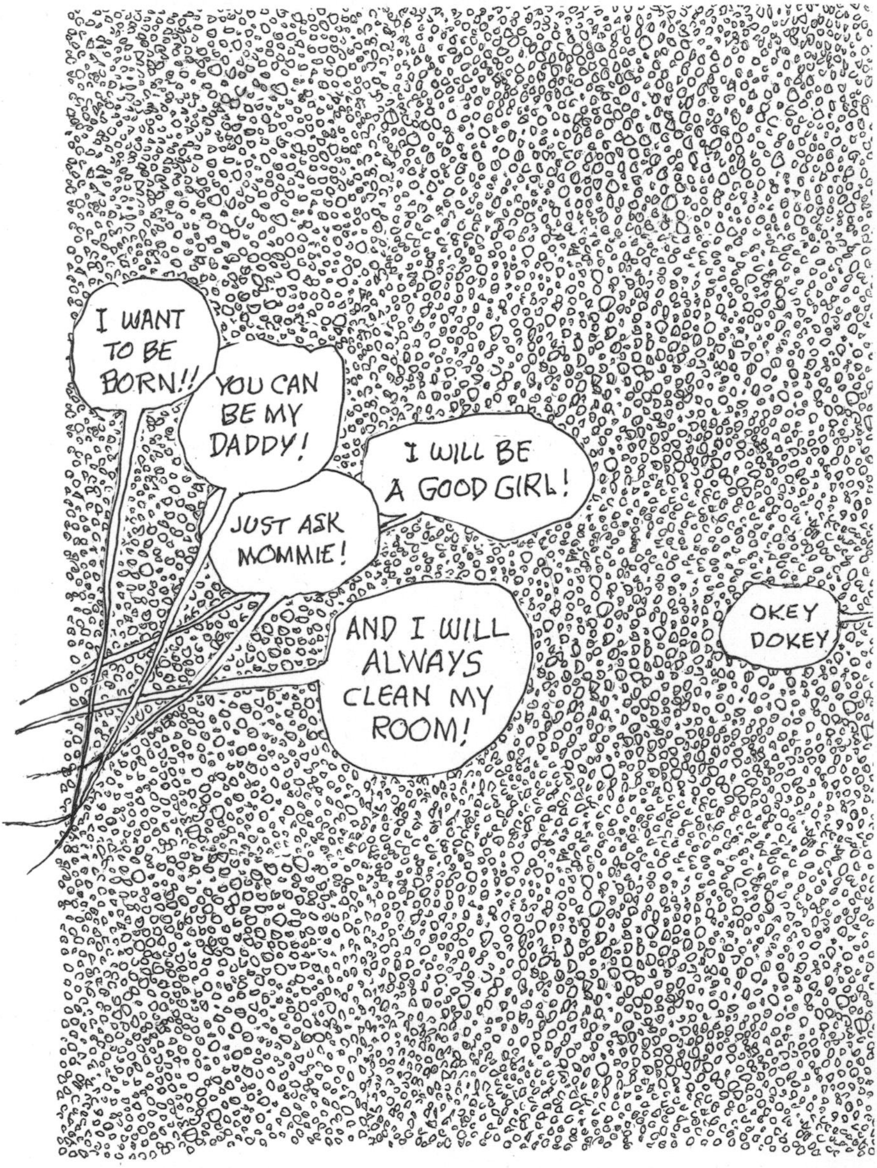
I WANT TO BE BORN!!
YOU CAN BE MY DADDY!
I WILL BE A GOOD GIRL!
JUST ASK MOMMIE!
AND I WILL ALWAYS CLEAN MY ROOM!
OKEY DOKEY

CHILDREN AREN'T YOUR FRIENDS

I've tried to make our children my friends. But I found out right away it doesn't work, because friends that I've had, I remember, they had jobs, and any friend I loaned money to became a non-friend, because they wouldn't pay it back, and after a while I just stopped talking to them. But that was a good thing.

You can't do that with children. You have to talk to them for the rest of your life.

When I used to drive, I recall driving my kids to school one day, and they asked me to stop the car two blocks away. I asked why. They said their friends were making fun of them because they were riding in a nice car.

Why can't these kids riding in the backseat defend me? I feed them, I clothe them, I buy them presents, many times against my own best wishes. And yet they don't have enough love for me to defend me against what their peers are saying about them riding in a nice car.

I bought a nice car for myself. I didn't buy a car that my children's peers would find acceptable. I'm really sorry that I didn't. (No, I'm not.)

Anyway, my children asked me if I would stop the car two blocks away from the school so they could walk and not be seen in the car with me. We live approximately eighteen miles from school. I've driven them every day, but now they tell me I have to let them out two blocks from the school so they can prove they walked to school and their friends will not make fun of them. What did I say to them? Nothing. I made a U-turn and took them back a mile and a half. And then I said:

"Okay, get out. You can walk to school."

They started yelling and screaming:

"We want to talk to Mom!"

Thank God this was before cell phones.

"Hey, man," I told them, "this is my car. You don't have a car. And first of all, none of you happen to have jobs. You're not earning any money. And out of the goodness of my heart I drop you off at school. And even though the state is protecting you, there isn't anything that says I must drop you off wherever you want me to drop you off. So I'm going to let you off here and you can walk a mile and a half to school and I'll stay far enough behind so your friends will never know I watched you."

So I made them get out. I could see them arguing, and obviously someone was mad because they started shoving each other. I watched them argue for maybe four minutes. Then I drove up and I said:

"What are you doing?"

They were blaming each other—it was her fault, no his fault, etcetera—so I said:

"Get in the car."

Which they did. And I asked:

"Do I have to stop two blocks away?"

"No, no, no, we'll go, we'll go."

So we drove up to the school and I said:

"Wait, not yet. Stay in the car."

I got out and I walked around and I made an announcement:

"My name is Bill Cosby and these are my children, and I want everybody to know that this is not their car. This is *my* car. And I have offered to be their chauffeur, and if anybody wants to make fun of them because they have a chauffeur, well, why don't you talk to your parents; maybe they will chauffeur you around."

The children got out of the car and for about five or ten steps they looked like those people on the five o'clock news who were being arrested. They were really trying to crawl and hide.

They didn't talk to me for about two days. I mean, it wasn't nasty; they were just very quiet.

I said, "How are your friends?"

I didn't get any answers at all. Which was fine with me. Because that was the last I wanted to hear anything about peer pressure. If you've got peer pressure, have your peers pick up the tab.

MY OWN ROOM

As a father, I always felt I had to protect my daughters against the nasty boys coming after them. But your daughter is the first one to tell you to back off.

"Daddy, I like him."

"I don't care."

Next thing you know, your wife is telling you:

"Listen, you have to stop sitting in the living room bothering people."

That's when you get another room. Buried someplace down in the basement. People coming and going but you don't know who anybody is. When someone asks me, "Who came over to your house?" the only way I can answer is to say, "I have no idea who anybody was. They wouldn't let me see anyone."

See, fathers know nothing. Because a father has been taught by his wife, the mother of the children, *You keep out of this!*

And if you're a father, and you stay in the house long enough, you will hear her tell the children:

Don't worry about it. I'll take care of him.

And the "him" she's talking about? That would be you.

MY SINGLE DAUGHTER

I have a daughter who is single. We were sitting and talking when a name came up. It was a professional basketball player. When I told her that he was a multimillionaire, she said she'd like to meet him. But when I said he was married, she said, "I really didn't want to meet him anyway. I was just joking."

And I said, "I would love for you to meet a basketball player who is making around four million, one hundred thousand dollars a year. And if he had his head together and was putting money away, you and me, we could put the money thing aside."

She said, "Dad! *Please!*"

I said, "I'm just talking, you know, like, information. I'm not pushing you anywhere. I don't see why you can't discuss this. I mean, it's not like I'm asking you to get married. I'm just saying, from my viewpoint—"

She cut me off and said, "You just seem to be interested in the money aspect."

I said, "Well the money *is* big."

"Dad!"

"But the money *is* huge because of the way you like to live. I know you and I know how you've been living."

"Oh, Dad! Please stop! This is so depressing."

And I said, "Yes, for both of us. I want you to understand that I feel I should be able to answer questions as opposed to being cut off. So, to answer your question—"

She said, "I've forgotten the question."

And I said, "Of course you have, because it's not on your tab. I just want you to realize that when you meet people, friends or whatever, you should consider what the monetary participation would be, would *have* to be, because of what you're accustomed to."

What I didn't say was *And how you don't participate in chipping in on monetary things, you know, like, to get a job.* I didn't say that. I said this:

"All I'm saying is, it would be nice if this fellow, whoever you meet, had some money. But then I would want you, of course, to be happy. Which means an awful lot of things. His behavior, his manners, his obedience toward you, which husbands need to learn, and they have to be taught like you train a dog or a parakeet. And eventually, if the female figures he's worth it, she'll keep him and keep training him. And, if he loves her, then he will comply and accept all of these rules and regulations and become a very quiet person who smiles and listens to his wife and doesn't mind getting up and moving to another room so that drapes can be changed and different pieces of furniture can be moved because it's that time of year."

When I looked up she was gone.

MY SON'S FIRST
BAD WORD

When my son Ennis was about seven years old he came into my office looking somewhat unhappy. I say "somewhat" because seven-year-old people don't really have a sustained expression of anything except mood changes. In other words, they're either running, jumping, rushing, yelling, or defending themselves with a look of defense on their face.

So Ennis came in seeming to be a shade confused and he said, "Dad?"

"Dad" with a question mark.

Before I could respond he raised his hand to shoulder height, turned the back of it to me, and lifted his middle finger. He then asked, "Is this a bad word?"

I told him yes it was. He took his right hand—he's left-handed—moved it to the hand with the raised finger, then folded the finger down and walked away.

RAISE YOUR
TAIL!

I have a five-year-old grandson. And the child somehow, through his mother, has gotten into a form of
violence — the violence of the tai chi. It seems his
mother has put him in a tai chi class. When he comes
home from the class, he has on the white outfit with the
white belt. He puts his hands together like coming in
peace, two palms meeting. He bows. And then he kicks
and punches the air, making this sound — *haah!* His
opponent is invisible, so I assume tai chi means "to beat
up an invisible person." I don't know who the person is
that he's fighting — I never bothered to ask. Kick —
haah! Punch — *haah!* You're looking at this child —
haah, haah, haah — with no reality in sight. Just fighting
someone invisible. Then, all of a sudden, it's *haah, haah,
haah* — all over me. He knows that in our home, the
home of the grandparents, he is not to hit any furniture
or glass or anything, even wood. Nothing. Pillows? No,
you don't hit the pillows.

My five-year-old grandson is absolutely delirious about Godzilla. He's always saying to me: "I have a new *Godzilla*, Grandpoppy! Do you want to watch it with me?"

I'm not a fan of Godzilla. It isn't that I don't like Godzilla, but for me, there is a genuine disconnect, at age seventy-three, to a large green lizard. My heroes, when it came to scaring me to death, were Boris Karloff and Lon Chaney. Lon Chaney had facial hair and wore a Brooks Brothers suit that was too small and a shirt where the cuffs were too long. He had an overbite. Horrible overbite. I also remember the eeriness of Dracula standing on the lawn of Lord So-and-So in front of an old castle.

And then there was King Kong. Not Mighty Joe Young, because they played "Beautiful Dreamer," and that was the end of that. You can't get scared when you hear "Beautiful Dreamer." It's like singing cowboys. Nor do I want my monsters to be calmed by soothing music. Frankenstein lost me when he started smoking cigars and listening to violins. I want to make it clear that I didn't enjoy him when he killed the little girl, but he *was* scary, and to this day, as of this writing, I am still frightened while laughing at the same time when seeing Frankenstein. I did not know that a human being was capable of being scared, frightened, and still able to laugh, not in hysteria, but laugh at comedy. When Lou

Costello sat on Frankenstein's lap, not knowing it was Frankenstein, I have never had such an epiphany. Nowhere have I seen anything that equaled that.

The first time I heard about *King Kong*, the movie, it was playing in the Booker movie house. We didn't have money in our home for me to go to a first-run showing, so I wound up going to the ten-cent edited-down version. Actually, *King Kong* was made in 1933, four years before I was born, in 1937. But at the time it came to the Booker, everybody was talking about it like it was the first time it ever was shown. We just didn't know any better.

I think for me the scene that almost had me up and running out of the theater—which people used to do in those days, they'd run out of the theater, and some people didn't use the aisles—was when he tore down that elevated train. That was the one that almost got me up from my seat and all the way out of the theater. Now, when I think back, I remember that you could, as you got older, eventually tell that the quote-unquote "pygmies" in the King Kong movie were actually white short people with black makeup all over and black legs. After that, it wasn't so frightening because those white short people with black makeup drew my attention away from the scariness.

Before you caught on about the pygmies, it was, in fact, a scary movie, and you went home with that movie in your head and you couldn't sleep. I would even hear grown people talking about a sleepless night because of King Kong. Or a sleepless night because of Frankenstein, a sleepless night because of Wolf Man. So those were my scare heroes.

I don't even know how word came to the projects, but at some point I heard about a movie called *Frankenstein Meets the Wolf Man*. And we, at the age of nine or ten or eleven, began arguing over who was the strongest, Frankenstein or Wolf Man. There were guys, boys that I was playing with—for example, Fat Albert, Rudy, and the gang—who said that Frank and Wolf Man were going to have this fight. This was before Ali and Frazier, so Frankenstein versus Wolf Man was all we had. And word was that this fight was definitely going to happen.

Everybody was rooting for Frank because Frank was bigger. But there was one guy who thought that Wolf Man, with his sharp teeth, could win because Frank's equilibrium wasn't that great. The guy kept saying that Wolf Man could move, he could feint, he could jump around, he was a wolf, he could go in and come out before Frank could close his hands around him. Still, everybody agreed that if Frank ever got his hands on Wolf Man, being a monster that couldn't feel pain, it wouldn't make any difference what Wolf Man bit off— Frank would continue.

Then, of course, when they showed the movie, there

was the wonderful ending of the two of them just fighting and then collapsing, and I think they both fell into something. They fell into an ice thing and they froze to death. Well, they were both dead anyway, but they froze so that the sequel comes and they thaw them out. Or it could have been a flood that killed them. Whatever. Those things are just a part of one's memories. Like a song that you couldn't get five people to buy today: "I'll Take You Home Again, Kathleen."

Since the grandchildren can watch this Godzilla thing stomp Japanese people to death, I decided to play *Frankenstein Meets the Wolf Man* for the grandchildren. This was after I put on an Abbott and Costello and they were bombing badly. The granddaughter and the grandson saw nothing funny in them. When they saw the monsters, it just did not register. So I played *Frankenstein Meets the Wolf Man*. I think they had an attitude like: *And you say this is supposed to be scary?* Knowing that I had an audience that was just trying to be nice to their grandfather, I turned it off and released them. They were very quick to leave.

By the same token, *Godzilla* is just not doing it for me. I also understand that Godzilla is female because this is what I'm told by my grandson. My wife and my daughter, the mother of the five-year-old, have also declared that Godzilla is female, but they also say this about God, so I'm not too sure.

"You are <u>not</u> Godzilla!"

One day we all went shopping. Actually, I was not shopping. The women, they went someplace and they put me with the grandson. We're in a store, a huge warehouse, which I cannot name. All I can say is that you can find everything in the world there except antiaircraft guns.

I, as a usual male, am looking for the furniture department so I can go over and pretend I'm going to buy an armchair. My grandson and I are walking along when he points to a DVD area. Not just an area, but a football field–sized part of the store with DVDs going all the way up to the ceiling. Now, out of a thousand million DVDs he spots the Godzilla rack. And on his own, without a great deal of excitement, he just runs and pulls the Godzilla DVD out and shows it to me and says:

Oh, Grandpoppy, a new Godzilla DVD!

And he says this clearly when other times he knows only words that have one syllable. Yes. No. Please. But now a sentence. And then more whole sentences:

Grandpoppy, I got a new one! Come on, you can watch it with me! It's Godzilla.

He holds up the *Godzilla* DVD, and I say, "Son, let me take a look." I'm thinking maybe they made a new Godzilla movie. On the front of the packaging is a drawing of Godzilla walking. And there are buildings, always lining a main street somewhere. The people are running toward the viewer—they're in the forefront, and Godzilla is behind, chasing them.

Just looking at the DVD cover, I couldn't understand what the story was about. From what I can see,
people are running and they're all scared. So I read the
back of the cover, and the story is very, very familiar to
me. And after I read the story on the back, it appears to
me that this is the same Godzilla movie he already has.
Only the picture on the front is different. So I say to
him, my five-year-old grandson, "You already have
this one."

Whereupon he shakes his head and looks up at me:

"No, no, no! No, no, no, Grandpoppy! I don't have
this one!"

"Yes, you do, you already have this one."

"No, no, no, look, the people on the front, I don't
have the people."

And now he starts to "no, no, no" over me and he's
working on tears and a little bit of loudness and a lot of
talking over Grandpoppy.

"Buy it, please, Grandpoppy! I don't have this one!
Please, Grandpoppy!"

So I do what I used to do when raising his mother
and that is to say, "Look at me," at least seventeen times
in a row, just back to back. *Look at me, look at me, look at
me*, rapidly following each other. After a while it kind of
strings together, goes into the child's brain area and
begins to freeze them. You can see them trying not to
look. But it's freezing them.

Now I'm saying "look at me" over and over to my grandson. I can tell it's freezing him because it pulls him around to where he's actually looking at me but he can't understand what I'm saying because now it's like:

Lookatmelookatmelookatme!

I'm jamming his thought waves, have frozen his little brain. It's a wonderful technique I've developed:

Lookatmelookatmelookatme!

And then I go:

Listentomelistentomelistentome!

And he's completely frozen. He's looking at me and his mouth is open. It's not that he's hypnotized; it's just that I've got his brain locked and he can't go to the begging part of his brain, or to the part where he's not listening. And I say:

You already have this. Youalreadyhaveit! Youalready-haveit! Youalreadyhaveit! Youalreadyhaveit!

And I can see him trying to say something, his head starting to go into a "no," but I kept jamming him:

Youhaveityouhaveityouhaveityouhaveit!

Now that he's frozen, I try to explain:

"All they did was put a different picture on the same one."

And then it broke — I lost him. And he's "no, no, no," and he's crying and he's very sad. Whereupon I say to him very loud, "Listen to me! This is a different drawing. The people know what they're doing by putting a different picture on the box. They're tricking you. You're only five years old. You've only been on this earth five years and you don't know how to read."

And I turn it over and I say, "See these words? If you could read, you'd know that these words say: You've already seen this movie before. We just have a different front for you."

He still didn't get it.

So now it's Halloween; the grandchildren have come to our home in Massachusetts to go trick-or-treating. When I was a child living in the Richard Allen projects with my parents, low-income parents, we had no money for costumes. The only costume I remember was putting lipstick on and then putting a pillowcase or sheet over the coat or something and going as...I don't know what I was going as. Costumes for kids whose parents have no money always involved a pillowcase or a sheet. But you couldn't cut holes in it because the sheet had to come back and be put on that bed again. So you take the sheet and it is tied around you and fixed in such a way according to how creative your mother and father happen to be. So maybe I went trick-or-treating as a sheet. What you can do with a sheet without putting holes in it: You can make a cape. And you can be a ghost. But you can't see through it. So you put the sheet over your head. You go up to somebody's door and you knock and then you put the sheet over yourself. And you say ooooh. And people smile. Then you take a handful of candy. You have your own bag, a brown paper bag. And I remember the candy got all mixed up, the salt with sweet or whatever was in the bag.

Today a kid gets a Godzilla costume on the Internet for fifty dollars. And the grandson has a Godzilla outfit,

obviously. The Godzilla claws are like gloves, and the same for the feet. Then there's the body and the head. And there's this tail, which you have to tie around the child's waist. The only flaw in all of it is if, while in the suit, he has to bend over, you can see his street clothing. Which, to my grandson, is embarrassing. He just did not want to show that. He was adamant about being Godzilla — not a kid in a Godzilla suit — but the real Godzilla. And with that costume on, he made the exact sound of Godzilla.

In a way, sort of, I just felt sorry for the kid, because this is all he has in his five-year-old life — just walking around with this thing on, this Godzilla costume. But as we walked, people actually stopped to take a picture of him. But he wouldn't make the sound, the Godzilla sound, even when people asked him to make it. I guess he wanted to make that sound only when *he* wanted to, not when grown people asked him to. Meanwhile, I didn't stand in the picture. I didn't want to be a part of it. Here I am walking with the grandson, and he's Godzilla. Everything he is, that looks like him, is covered up with this rubber green and silver color. And I'm looking at the rubber feet and the rubber hands of Godzilla and thinking: *This is my grandson?*

We walk up to this door and we knock on it and people open it and he starts with this noise. Authentically scary and scaly. Now, because his outfit is so complete, they didn't give him anything to put the candy in, so I was the person they gave the candy to. I held the bag, he made the noise again, and then they closed the door, acting real scared.

As we walked around, there were some people who didn't realize it, but they stepped on his tail by mistake. This would pull him down and make him very, very upset. So I said to him, "Yes, son, you are a scary monster but there are some problems with being Godzilla. People step on your tail."

CABBAGE PATCH

In the early 1980s, they came out with a thing called the Cabbage Patch doll. It was, to me, with its distorted face, one of the ugliest things I have ever seen, ever. A horrible, gruesome-looking thing. But that didn't matter. In the minds of millions of children in America and around the world, the "I want" part of their brain went off.

Now, this was before social networking. As I write this piece in the year 2011 I wonder, if social networking had been available back then, what might have happened. Someone could have seen the dolls on a social-networking site and started counterfeiting them. Or maybe people would have written about how ugly this thing was and it wouldn't have taken off. Because, as you can see on today's social-networking pages, there's an awful lot of profanity from an awful lot of people who seem to be very angry about something, although they may at times even make sense.

On the other hand, social networking could have tripled the maniacal "I want" of the children, and all kinds of things could have broken loose. We'll never know. All we know is that through a commercial or whatever — I don't remember Cabbage Patch commercials, but there must have been commercials — children heard about Cabbage Patch dolls and insanity broke out. An epidemic. The number of authentic Cabbage Patch dolls in each family — I think it came out to something like ninety-three million. Three times the population of Canada.

With some of the most gruesome faces I've ever seen, I don't think anybody really loved these things as much as they just wanted to have them because somebody else had them. If only children were allowed to drive, they could have made the Edsel a huge success.

What happened with the Cabbage Patch dolls proved that, even without the Internet, the behavior of children can create a mass "I want." One child says "I want" because another child says "I want," and so forth and so on. And so this is really the expected behavior of a child: "I want." But what about the behavior of people in charge of children? These are the people who really went way over the behavioral normal. Their behavior, to use another word, was not *usual* behavior.

Over the years, I've grown tired of people telling me

what is normal or usual. Sometimes, when I pointed out that something was not normal, people would challenge me:

Well, what is usual? Where do we have normal?

Well, normal is when you're coming down the street and people are coming from the opposite direction and nobody speaks and nobody smiles. That's normal. What is not normal is walking down the street and looking at somebody, somebody you've never seen before, and this person smiles and nods as he walks by. That's not normal.

To get on an elevator, four people are already standing there, and everybody's pretending that they're focused on the numbers, there's no eye contact—that's usual behavior. Not usual is when a person gets on an elevator with five other people, and nobody knows anybody, but then this person, whom you've never seen before in your life, makes eye contact and smiles. The person doesn't want you romantically, doesn't want long conversation, just kind of nods, and you nod back, and then you both go back to your numbers.

So I find that the word "usual" usually drives people away from what is usual. And usually the normal behavior after that is they argue about what is normal. But usually, as you go along and you look at things, you can throw the word "normal" around so they won't catch it enough to challenge your normal. Or you can be prepared as I have prepared myself to defend normal. And then you get to abnormal.

To make them understand abnormal is very easy to do. You're in a room, sitting, and a person comes into the room. You're the only person in the room, and that other person just stands there and smiles at you. Every time you look up that person is still looking at you and smiling. That's abnormal. And it will draw you out of your comfort zone into a number of emotions: fear, anger, and all the words in a thesaurus.

If they still don't understand what abnormal behavior is, all you have to do is have someone attack them. Abnormal behavior is somebody coming in and you're just sitting down and they start hitting you over the head with a bottle. And you'll find that people have no counter for that; they'll agree that someone hitting someone over the head with a bottle is abnormal. Then you'll say to them, *Okay, now what do you consider normal?* And leave that up to them. Usually they'll take their discussion away because they didn't really want to get that deep. Especially about themselves. Plus, they don't want to be hit in the head with a bottle.

The actions of the parents of children who wanted the Cabbage Patch doll was not usual, not normal; it was abnormal. They called it a frenzy. It was worse than that. It was grown people freeing themselves from all behavior of usualness. Deep-rooted things came out of human beings. People hurt other people. Yes, I've seen and heard about big sales, 20 percent off or whatever. And I am well aware of mob violence, people following the mob mentality, getting caught up in things.

I remember when word came that World War II had ended, and I remember being near the Booker Movie. And some kid was yelling, "The war is over and you can get in the Booker Movie for free." Running when he said it—like he had found a hundred dollars. So a mob formed. But the owner or manager of the Booker Movie stopped this foolishness immediately by closing the door and standing out front. He didn't even have security guards. He just closed the door and locked it and went into the booth that sells the tickets and yelled:

"This is not true. You cannot get in for free. It's eight cents a ticket! It is not free. Congratulations on the war. The war is over. Now, all of you go home and get your eight cents."

And it turned the mob around. Nobody was angry. They just said, "It's not free, but the war is over."

But nothing stopped the parents who wanted a Cabbage Patch doll for (as they claimed) their children.

It reminds me of when Jack Benny was confronted by a robber who put a gun in his back and said, "Your money or your life!" And Benny said nothing for a long,

long time, maybe thirty seconds. So the robber repeated his demand: "Your money or your life!" And Benny said, "I'm thinking, I'm thinking."

What were these mothers thinking? Whom did these people really buy this ugly doll for? What puts you in such a dire position of parenting that you absolutely have got to have this thing for your child? I want to walk away from the easiest explanation: that the doll was not for the child but it was for you. I also want to walk away from the easy one, which is you want to buy something that will make your child love you. No, I want to get into the complex reasons why you stormed the store.

So what was it that the doll represented to you? Why did this doll, this "thing" or "symbol" or whatever a psychiatrist might call it, cause you to look at these other people in the store as if they were your enemies? You parents stormed and fought and tore materials and boxes.

I will buy this because my child must have this!

And the mothers turned into witches from *The Wizard of Oz.* Or vicious queens shouting: "Off with their heads!" Rules changed.

Actually, there were no rules.

I saw it first!

Yes, but I got to it before you did!

Was it really love that drove people to this? I don't think so. There was no law. Women fought and clawed.

The fairer sex? The little lady? The *weaker* sex? Hogwash!

Anybody with any sense or anyone who has ever watched the Discovery Channel realizes that there's nothing weak about the female. For example, the female praying mantis, after sex, will bite the head off of the male. And I've never heard of a father bear tearing up some human being who got too close to the cubs. Okay, once in a while you'll hear of a father bear tearing up some people who caught him going through their trash or busting open a locked freezer to get at frozen steaks. But basically all a father bear does is just sit on the river-bank and smack fish. Smacks salmon as they're flying by. That's about it. And then he goes to sleep.

Whoever made up this weaker-sex thing forgot that you don't mess with a female anything. A female bird leaves the nest to scout an area where there are plenty of worms. And she has great eyesight from the air so she can also see human beings, or a snake, anything coming near her eggs or her young children. And she will attack. You don't go near a bird's nest when the baby birds are in there, because the mama bird will fly down on top of you. A bird can cause a hunter to drop the gun and run away. It doesn't have to be an eagle. And I'm not even talking about a crazed mother hawk. I'm talking about a wren. Even an upset mother wren can do damage. And they know exactly what to go for on a human being. They will go for your eardrum and take you out with that little beak.

Not long ago, Mrs. Cosby decided that we should have a bird feeder on our property. The birds fly into it and it has some wood sticking out for the birds to stand on. There are seeds inside, so the birds fly in and out. And it's a wonderful thought to know that in the dead of winter you have this thing outside that's feeding birds. You feel like you're part of nature.

So I hung this nice wooden house for the birds on a branch, and pretty soon I found out that we had a blue jay in our area. Now, the blue jay, according to word of mouth, is a nasty, take-no-prisoners kind of bird. This bird is afraid of nobody.

One day, a squirrel came by and saw the bird feeder. It must have been a pretty smart squirrel because he immediately realized he could climb the tree, go out on the branch, eat the bird's food, then jump out and go back on the branch.

This did not sit well with the blue jay.

What happened next, as I stood and watched, was one of the most bizarre events ever to occur in nature. If I hadn't seen it for myself, and known what it was, I would have been unable to describe it and would have just said it was the strangest flying thing I had ever seen.

I saw the squirrel come down, work its way down to the feeder, and start eating the seeds meant for the birds. And I was not the only one seeing this. The blue jay was watching too.

I don't know for sure if it was the mother blue jay or the father blue jay—I can't tell the difference between a male and female blue jay—but whichever it was made a pass, saw the squirrel eating the seeds, then came around to the back entrance where the squirrel was hunched over with his tail up.

Well, the blue jay dives straight at the squirrel, and the blue jay's head went right in. In other words, it was a giant goosing. A spectacular, never-been-seen-before, headfirst goosing.

The reaction of the squirrel was to leap off the feeder, with the head of the blue jay intact. Now the blue jay and the squirrel were airborne, with the blue jay's head and shoulders inside the orifice of the squirrel. The blue jay started flapping its wings and soared back up to about seventy feet. It looked like the weirdest bird I had ever seen.

At an altitude of eighty or ninety feet, the blue jay dropped the squirrel into a wooded area. As the squirrel plummeted to the ground, the blue jay made a starboard

banked turn, flew to a birdbath (which Mrs. Cosby also had me buy) and took a total bath. I could hear calls from different trees, and although I knew it had to be my mind, I swear I thought I could hear other birds applauding this blue jay. And I could hear woodpeckers pecking on the tree trunks in such perfect time, the Florida A&M drummers would have been very proud.

To this day I have never seen another squirrel near that bird feeder. Although I did see other birds circling, and there was one bird that somebody said looked like a loon. A loon? It looked like a duck to me. But that got me to wondering what a loon was. I'd heard expressions like "crazy as a loon" and words like "loony bin." But why was this bird used to describe something crazy? So I went to the computer and started searching.

According to Wikipedia: "The loon is the size of a large duck or small goose, which it resembles in shape when swimming. Like ducks and geese, but unlike coots and grebes, the loon's toes are connected by webbing."

Coots? Like an "old coot"? What is a "coot"?

Well, more searching turned up the fact that a coot is a medium-sized water bird, but it didn't say anything about why the word "coot" refers to an old person. And I still didn't know why loons are crazy. Back to Wikipedia: "Flying loons resemble a plump goose with a seagull's wings, relatively small in proportion to the bulky body."

Resembling a plump goose could make you crazy. But there had to be another reason.

"Male and female loons have identical plumage."

Aha! They can't tell each other apart! That could be enough to make you crazy. But then I finally found out the real reason for the expression "crazy as a loon." Apparently, the loon makes a weird, laughing call that sounds like a crazy person.

But wait! A very scholarly friend of mine pointed out a passage from Shakespeare's *Winter's Tale*: "These dangerous unsafe lunes i' the king, beshrew them!"

My friend said that the word "lune," in Shakespeare's time, was short for "lunatic."

Since Adam named all the animals, and Adam was way before Shakespeare, I'm going with the weird, laughing sound.

Anyway, we were talking about females in the animal kingdom. But what about human females? And this is not to say that somebody set up a law where the male marries a female several years younger than he is. But that does happen often. Which means that later on you get to die before she does because you're older than she is. It isn't always the case, but females do tend to outlive the male, stick around ten, twenty years longer than the male. So all this weaker-sex stuff is just not true.

But I digress.

Let's get back to the women who descended on the department store. When last seen, they were tearing into boxes and throwing things while they tried to grab one of these dolls. Who were these people, really?

And why did the department store allow this kind of behavior? What department store manager sits in a meeting and says to his staff:

I want something in here that, when we open the doors, is going to cause people to trample our merchandise and beat up our salespeople. It'll be great for the business.

What do the department-store people think all these years later? Is it a wonderful memory? Or a painful one?

And the price of these dolls? I don't know what the original price was, but today, when you look them up on eBay, they're, like, fifty dollars. And somewhere in this world, there's got to be at least three hundred people with injuries that they will—as old people say—go to the grave with. Broken limbs. Scars. Dislocated joints. And all over this ugly doll with a certificate that says, "Hi, my name is" and so forth and so on.

And what about the children that cried and screamed (like a loon) for these ugly dolls? Whose mothers went out, the human being mother went out, and took on hundreds of other human being mothers. These children now have to be at least twenty years old. Do they even remember what their parents went through to satisfy the "I want" part of their brain? I don't think so. And when these mothers look back on these scars, physical and emotional, do they think it was worth it?

My wife and I have argued about these dolls. She thinks the pet rock was even worse.

THEY SHOULD DO THIS
EVERY THREE MONTHS

Each year, the grandchildren and their parents come to our home in Massachusetts for Christmas. We are in the central part of the state, north of Springfield, so we live in an area of farmland.

I have heard U.S.-born people describe their first trip to Africa with the word "stink." You have to remember, Africa is not the zoo. These animals are the indigenous animals. So if you are downwind, you will get a strong scent. The reason I'm saying this is for people to understand that we live in the dairy-farm part of Massachusetts. Many cows. And on a given summer day, with some four hundred cows, you will get a whiff of whatever those cows happen to be doing. Welcome to non-Africa, USA.

To get to our home, one comes off the interstate, and then there are fourteen miles of inland driving. Roads that have been smoothed out by wagons, cars, flat-footed elk, and heavy-pawed mountain lions. Trails of things that either travel in herds or packs or all those groups that animals and birds and fish travel in. Like a school of rabbits.

No, no, that's fish.

And over the years there have been a gaggle of geese, a herd of cattle, and a pride of pigs — no, no, that's lions.

But anyway, the road has been flattened out, not so much by man, but by wheels and paws. I suspect there has even been a thing of turkeys along these roads. What do you call a thing of turkeys? A flock? No, that makes no sense because flocks fly. Yes, flocks fly far. And I have seen few turkeys flying either near or far. So I looked it up and found out a thing of turkeys is called a rafter. A rafter of turkeys. And the very day that I was writing this piece, I said to my grandchild:

"A thing of turkeys is not a flock; it's called a rafter. A rafter of turkeys."

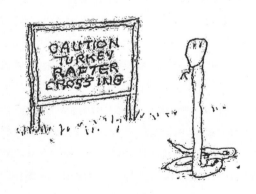

And this seven-year-old female just kept walking and muttering something like: "Grandpoppy has lost it again."

Then she went to my wife, who is Grandma, and said to her, "Grandpoppy is making up things again."

My wife, who is the wordsmith of the house, without even being asked, came to me to find out why the grandchild had said "Grandpoppy is making things up again."

Don't ever make a mistake when you are using words with my wife. It's better just to draw pictures. Because if you say anything to my wife, she will seek first of all to find out if you are using a real word or if it is not a real word. Then you can pronounce it two or three different ways, after which she will leave the dinner table and dig around to find out everything there is to know about that word.

So when I, through research, learned that a thing of turkeys is actually called a rafter, and then the grandchild went to my wife and said, "Grandpoppy is making things up again," my wife came to me and said, "What are you teaching the children?"

Well, I could've seized the moment and attacked her by saying, "That is plural."

And then she would say, "What is plural?"

My response would be: "You said 'children.' There's only one child that I've spoken to."

And then she would say one word: "Look!"

And that wipes out everything I have ever done or said in my life.

She had asked me, "What are you teaching the children?" So I answered. "A thing of turkeys is called a rafter."

She immediately turned around and left the room. After a few minutes, she came back, and then she made a sound that I have only heard in movies when Native Americans are getting ready to speak English.

She said, "Hmmm."

And I knew I was correct. Whenever I hear "hmmm," I know I must be right.

Then she said, "Well it, doesn't *sound* correct."

Obviously, she was making up for the child saying I had lost it. Then she said, "You've got the reputation of being a mountain of misinformation."

And I said, "Well, is that the same as traveling with a rafter of turkeys?"

"Yes," she said. "When you are with your friends. That's what it is. A rafter of turkeys."

I could have come at her with a few more birds I found. Like a murmuration of starlings. A parliament of owls. A sedge of cranes. An exaltation of larks. Or even a convocation of eagles. And I could have switched to animals. A gang of elk. A clowder of cats. A leap of leopards. A shrewdness of apes. A mute of hounds. Yes, I could've done that.

But I thought better of it.

Anyway, it's Christmas Eve and we're at the house with the grandchildren. We have, at the time of this writing, three grandchildren: two sevens and a five. The boy is five and, as you know from reading this book, he is obsessed with Godzilla. And he hums. I don't know if it's the theme song from *Godzilla*, but whatever it is, he walks around humming.

To protect the grandchildren, I will not give you the correct names. That's because, as of this writing, my wife has not agreed that it's all right to use the grandchildren's names. So I will do something I have often done in my past. I will give these people nicknames. And these nicknames may not have anything to do with the names given to them at birth. To me a nickname can be because of what the person looks like or sounds like—in a Damon Runyonesque way.

Three grandchildren. The two girls are both seven. One shall be called Camille II, as in Camille Two or Camille the Second. The other one shall be called Lacey. And the five-and-nine-tenths-year-old boy shall be called G.P. Which is short for "growing pains." These kids have an energy and my wife loves these people, but they have decibels. When my wife said they were coming for Christmas again this year, I didn't say anything. That's because I am a husband for forty-six years. You pick your battles. And I have a long list of things that I have passed up.

Now, I love my grandchildren, but everything with

them is a matter of loud crying or loud laughing. We don't know many of the quiet moments unless they've found something for themselves and nobody else is bothering them. The girls appear to do fine when they're playing together and talking to dolls. But the boy is a loner. He walks around by himself making Godzilla noises.

However, it always seems that from the very room where the girls are playing nicely, I eventually hear a scream, which echoes all throughout the house:

G.P.! Stop it!

And then one of the girls will run out of the room crying, the decibels very high, crying and talking in a way that I can't understand anything she is saying. That's the problem with everybody who cries: You can't understand what anybody did to cause the crying.

As they cry and talk, it's almost as if they're about to collapse, especially when they hit the emotional, shrieking, "this is the worst thing ever in my life" wall.

Then, at some point, the crying and talking turn into anger, which causes the slamming of a door. In *my* house, not in their house, when they slam these doors, the vibration goes around and hits some other doors in the house. So, if a door slams on the second floor, doors on the first floor react. Some doors just kind of move back and forth and bang against the doorstop. Others close on their own just because of the door slamming on the second floor. So what we have is a slamming by a seven-year-old that creates a vortex that causes other doors that are not locked to move in solidarity. Some opening, some closing. So we keep having to remind these people not to slam doors.

On this particular day, when I heard *G.P.! Stop it!*, all I wanted to do was catch the *G.P.! Stop it!* scream before it became crying and the slamming of the doors. I went in the room and I saw that G.P. was caught. He had something in his hand that belonged to one of the girls, and she was about to cry. And the girl, Lacey, was loud. You see, before the crying, first comes the loud.

"G.P. took that and it's mine!"

She says this very, very loud.

G.P. comes to defend himself. He's looking at me, his mouth open, and I guess he had a great deal of hope that I would side with him. And he said, in a very loud voice, "She wouldn't let me play with this!"

I said, "Well, who does it belong to?"

He said something like, "I don't know who...she won't let me play with this!"

And he stayed with that, that it was her fault.

"I haven't done anything," G.P. insisted. "She won't let me play with this!"

And Lacey kept saying, "It's mine and you took it!"

And he said, "But you won't let me play with this!"

That was his defense. Over and over. There he was holding something that belongs to someone else and his defense consisted of: *Okay, it's hers and I have it. But she won't let me play with it!*

Just so you understand the brain of a five-year-old, let me explain this young man's ability to reason. I was sitting in that same room—it was not Christmas, it was not Easter, no holiday—the children had come for the summer to visit. G.P. and Lacey were there playing. And he was playing by himself, pretending to be a train conductor on his own train. Lacey noticed this and said, "G.P., I need you to be the conductor for my train."

He said he would do that. Three minutes later, she said, "G.P., I now need you to start as the conductor of my train."

And he said to her, "I'm sorry to tell you this, Lacey. But I won't be able to be your conductor."

He was just being nasty, and I knew that.

So Lacey said, "Then you're fired!"

G.P. dropped everything he was holding and turned into a crying, screaming child.

"She's being mean to me, Grandpoppy!"

I said, "Wait, wait, stop! I heard you say that you were sorry you couldn't be the conductor."

G.P. started crying and talking.

"Buk shir divint plash ma!"

"Look, G.P.," I said, "you had already quit. Why are you crying because she fired you?"

And he just kept crying and talking at the same time.

He never even said "She can't fire me." I just think he was upset because she, in a way, topped him.

Now, on this particular Christmas Eve, I received a call from one of Santa's helpers by the last name of Jones, who asked to speak with my grandchildren. I did not know, nor did I ask, how assistant Jones got my phone number. So I said, "Just a minute," and I gathered the children.

"An assistant of Santa Claus is on the phone. Her name is Miss Jones and she wants to talk to the three of you."

And they all did everything the same way at the same time. They walked into the room as if they were fused at the shoulders, all in the same position. Their heads dropped to look at the phone in the same way at the same time. I put the call on the speakerphone, which was on a leather chair, as it has always been. And they stared at the red light that said "speaker."

"Miss Jones," I said, "the children are all here."

"Hello," Miss Jones said.

Camille II, at age seven, was close to becoming an agnostic when it came to Santa Claus. But when she heard the voice of Miss Jones, her expression transformed to one I can only imagine an agnostic would have during a surprise visit from God.

And the expressions on the faces of the other two changed as well. There was a look in their eyes — their eyes all of a sudden appeared to look clearer. Their faces, when I said Santa Claus, an assistant of Santa Claus, they seemed to brighten. It wasn't a smile, it wasn't an expression of cheer; it was just a look as if they had been blessed. All of a sudden, I felt an aura coming from the three of them. Not that I could hear a thousand monks humming something Latin in unison, but it was obvious that they had gone into some sort of reverent zone. They just stood there in silence, saying nothing, their mouths slightly parted. And they blinked—it wasn't a fast blink or a slow one. Just a blink. These children were in a trance. It was like the people doing tai chi in Chinatown when they stared at the tree and held the position. Then the children's heads turned down to look at the phone. And they never even registered that I was there.

Miss Jones asked, "Is Lacey there?"

And Lacey answered in a Gregorian tone, "Yeeeesss."

Miss Jones, Santa's assistant, said, "I have your list and I just want to go over it with you."

Lacey did not breathe. She just, with her mouth partially open, kept looking at the red light on the phone that said "speaker."

As Miss Jones went over the list, the child Gregorian-ed:

"Yeeeesss."

"Yeeeesss."

"Yeeeesss."

And then she went to the second grandchild.

"Who is Camille Two?"

And Camille II also answered in this Gregorian chant–like voice, "I ... aaaaam ... Caaaamille ... Twoooo ..."

Then Miss Jones said, "Good. I'm going over *your* list. Are these the things you asked for?"

"Yeeeesss."

"Yeeeesss."

"Yeeeesss."

When Miss Jones finished with the two girls, she said, "G.P."

And G.P., who is five, tilted his head toward the ceiling, and he said, "I have been naughty. But as of the last three days I have been very nice."

And I thought, this is just wonderful. Here is this five-year-old boy cleaning up his act. Confessional lying. The boy will admit to a few bad things because he believes Santa knows everything but then comes back with a few good things from the last couple of days.

"The good one is here in Massachusetts."

"Yes," Miss Jones said. "I'm looking at film of your behavior over the last six months, and you have made some errors. But lately you have been stellar."

"What is that?"

"Stellar means better than good."

"Yeeeesss," G.P. said. "The last three nights I have

been very nice to . . . to . . . to . . . to everyone." And then he said, "And God bless *you*!"

"Well, thank you," Miss Jones said. "I'll get this to Santa. And before I go, please be aware that you may get a call from Skyler, Santa's navigator."

Upon hearing that, the children went back to those trancelike expressions again.

I said, "Good night, Miss Jones."

"Nice talking to you, Mr. Cosby. I have all of your records."

"Thank you."

"And Santa wants to know when you're going to make a record about him."

"Soon. And I'll be nice."

"It's too late for you, buddy," Miss Jones said as she hung up.

The children walked out, still joined at the shoulder, as if they had been practicing these walks. I don't know if it was my imagination, but I swear I could hear Gregorian chants coming from the other room.

As Miss Jones had said, I then got a call from a person named Skyler, who said he had to speak to the children because he is routing Santa's travel with the reindeer. So I called the children and they came back in, shoulder to shoulder. Again, maybe I was imagining it, but it looked like somebody had put a bowl on G.P.'s head and cut his hair in the style of a Franciscan monk.

And they all went right back to those same Gregorian expressions again as they then dropped their heads and stared at the red light on the speakerphone.

"Mr. Skyler," I said. "The children are here."

"Very good. What are your names?"

And they never moved their heads when they answered.

"Lacey."

"Camille Two."

"G.P."

"I just want to know," Skyler said, "because I'm the fellow who guides Santa and the sled and all the presents and the reindeer, and we want to know exactly where your house is. Where are you?"

They said, in Gregorian unison, "We're in Massachusetts."

"Where is it in Massachusetts?" Skyler asked. "We don't understand where you are because there aren't any children living there, just people who can take care of themselves. Grandparents and aunties and uncles. They buy their own things. And they are generally awake when Santa gets there. So they want to talk, ask how Santa's wife is doing and have a long conversation. But Santa is channeled, he's working, and he just doesn't have that much time because he is very, very busy. He doesn't have time for chitchat. He's working and he doesn't want to be late. So, if there are no children, Santa crosses that house off his list. But because you are visiting Grandpoppy and Grandmommy, I need one of you children to tell me how to get to your house."

"You get off the plane," Camille II began, "and then you ride a long time."

"How long?"

"You fall asleep."

"Okay," Skyler said.

"And then," Camille II continued, "you wake up and you come to, you know, the circle. Be careful. If you miss the circle you'll go to Vermont."

She kept saying "you know," as if Skyler should know these landmarks in Massachusetts. And she started naming places on the way from the airport to the house. All the places she wanted to eat.

"And you go past, you know, Friendly's restaurant, and, you know, Taco Bell, and then you keep going, and after that...there's nothing after that."

"I don't know these places," Skyler said. "Which interstate is it?"

"It's the one in Massachusetts," Lacey said.

"Yes, but what is the number of the interstate?"

"It keeps changing," Camille II replied.

"What do you mean?"

"It used to be called 29."

"Is that the miles?"

Camille II was very quiet because she wasn't sure what to say. Finally, she said, in a very small voice, "Yeah."

"Then what do I do?"

"You go down past two farms," Camille II explained. "One with horses and one cows. That's our next-door neighbor. They have a lot of black cows. But when it's nighttime you can't really see them. You have to do a curve and then straight. And you'll see our house with the gate in front. You can tell it's Grandymommy and Grandpoppy's place because they have nothing. No cows. Just little children."

Skyler got the directions, but he was still rather confused about where the house was, so he asked them if they, right then, would go outside because he had a special television screen that could see all over the world. If they went outside and looked north, Skyler told them, he would be able to see them and then he could show Santa how to get there.

I went and got their parents. And their parents were smiling.

"You've got to hurry," Skyler said over the speakerphone, "because Santa is just about ready to take off. And I just want the children out there. No parents. And they have to look north."

So they all went out and their parents were yelling from inside, "Look north! Look north!"

And the three of them looked in three different directions.

"Tell them to point to the house," Skyler said.

"Point to the house!" their parents shouted from the doorway.

And they did. I could see they were really cold, but they didn't mind.

"I saw you," Skyler said when they came back in. "Now I have to go and explain to Santa where you live."

Just as they were leaving the room, shoulders fused, a third call came in. It was Santa's dietician. And his name was Stymie.

The grandchildren stood, focused, tai chi expression on their faces again, the most well-behaved people. And the Gregorian aura was back around them.

I put Stymie on the speakerphone and the children are standing there and staring at the red light and Stymie tells them that Santa, due to dietary restrictions, cannot have cookies and milk. And I never really thought about it, but by the time Santa gets to our house, he has eaten five thousand cookies and nine hundred pieces of cake. Which is probably why he hired a dietician. After years of eating all the things children have left out for him, Santa probably had a bad checkup and the doctor told him he had to watch what he ate.

"Please do not put cookies and milk down there," Stymie instructed the children.

So Lacey said, "I already made chocolate chip cookies for him."

"Santa cannot have them," Stymie insisted.

So I barged in and told Stymie, "You go ahead and eat them and drink the milk."

"How about Silk?" Camille II asked. "Soy milk."

"Santa doesn't like soy," Stymie replied. "He just wants a glass of water."

G.P. asked, "Bottled or the well?"

And Stymie said, "From the glass bottle."

And G.P. (remember, he's only five) said, "Okay, I will leave a glass bottle of water and an opener because you have to have a bottle opener for it. But leave the opener, don't take it, because a lot of people keep taking our openers."

"Okay," Stymie said, "you guys take it easy. Bye-bye."

The children left the room, fused at the shoulders once again. And quiet.

"I have never seen such good behavior," I said to Stymie.

And then the disembodied voice of Santa's dietician boomed over the speakerphone:

"Yeah, they should do this stuff every three months."

THE LAST WORD

I am told that the Louvre in Paris, one of the most famous art museums in all the world, has security stationed to look out for, and hopefully recognize, famous artists who are coming into the museum to look for their paintings. The guards are instructed to examine the pockets of the artists to make sure that they have no little jars or tubes of paint or any brushes hidden in their clothing. And if the artists do have brushes and paint, the guards confiscate these things so that the artists can't go inside and make changes to their works.

As of this particular writing, on this page, I now announce that there will be no further additions or subtractions or other mathematical equations. Thereto and wherefore and whereas, upon itself, I decree decryingly the last word.

mc   ⊩ ⫽